QUICK AND

# Vegan
# Celebrations

Over 150 Great-Tasting
Recipes Plus Festive
Menus for Vegantastic
Holidays and Get-Togethers
All Through the Year

Alicia C. Simpson

**THE EXPERIMENT**
NEW YORK

QUICK AND EASY VEGAN CELEBRATIONS:
*Over 150 Great-Tasting Recipes Plus Festive Menus for Vegantastic Holidays
and Get-Togethers All Through the Year*

Copyright © Alicia C. Simpson, 2010
Insert photographs © Lori Maffei, 2010

The Experiment, LLC
260 Fifth Avenue
New York, NY 10001-6425
www.theexperimentpublishing.com

Many of the designations used by manufacturers and sellers to distinguish their products are claimed as trademarks. Where those designations appear in this book and The Experiment was aware of a trademark claim, the designations have been capitalized.

The Experiment's books are available at special discounts when purchased in bulk for premiums and sales promotions as well as for fundraising or educational use. For details, contact us at info@theexperimentpublishing.com.

Library of Congress Control Number: 2010924702
ISBN 978-1-61519-022-5

Cover design by Susi Oberhelman
Cover photograph © Colin Cooke, featuring Jambalaya (page 78),
Key Lime Cupcakes (page 238), and Fresh-Squeezed Lemonade (page 156)
Author photograph by Kelly Donovan
Photo insert food styling and photography by Lori Maffei
Text design by Pauline Neuwirth, Neuwirth & Associates, Inc.

Manufactured in the United States of America

First published October 2010
Published simultaneously in Canada

10 9 8 7 6 5 4 3 2 1

*Dedicated to my baby brother, James.*
*I live every day of my life as a celebration of and tribute to yours.*

# Contents

# Party Starter or Party Pooper

**I**T IS NO secret that I love to eat. My love affair with food is all encompassing. I go to bed mapping out my breakfast options for the next morning. While eating breakfast I'm already picking out what my midday snack will be.

I tackle all holidays and celebrations with the same zeal. There's no way I'm going to an Independence Day cookout without a menu planned or at the very least a Boca burger, or two, and a bag of chips and some dip. I'm not the kind of girl who will ever sit shyly in the corner starving to death at a Thanksgiving dinner. My goal at any celebration is to bring as much scrumptious vegan food as humanly possible. Over time I've become famous for bringing my own plate to events, and as a result, my friends and family have started cooking up vegan options for me once they see how easy and delicious vegan food can be. Oftentimes I have to hurry up and get to the vegan options because they're usually the first to go.

A healthy, happy vegan is one of the best advertisements for a vegan lifestyle—so be a party starter and not a party pooper. Use this book as a guide not only to get the party started at your own vegan celebration but also to introduce fabulous vegan dishes to your friends and family.

# How to Get Your Party Started

**t**HERE IS A menu for each holiday and celebration in this book. These menus are flexible and designed to fit the needs of a small dinner party or gathering, all the way up to a large celebration with all your friends, family, and maybe even a couple of party crashers.

The key to pulling off a stress-free celebration is a strong game plan. Look over the celebration menu carefully, paying close attention to the serving sizes. For a small get-together, choose one or two main recipes and pair these foods with the dessert and cocktail of your choice. For a large jamboree, cook as few as three to four main items, or make the full menu, complete with desserts and cocktails.

Once you have your recipes picked out, take an inventory of your kitchen to make sure you have all the ingredients you will need for each. This will prevent a mad dash to the grocery store ten minutes before your guests arrive. Also, look for components of the recipe that you can make ahead. Chik'n Seitan (page 258) and Andouille Sausage (page 76), which are used in several recipes, can be made days ahead of time. Many recipes, such as Lime Sorbet with Mixed Berries and Chambord (page 69), Red Cabbage Salad (page 107), Taco Soup (page 136), and Chipotle Black Bean Burgers (page 140), taste even better the next day.

Most importantly, have fun. The best meals are those cooked with love. So turn your music up, put on your favorite apron, and don't be afraid to dance, sing, and sway as you cook up a celebration your guests will never forget.

# A Kitchen for All Occasions

**t**HERE'S NOTHING WORSE than being halfway into making a birthday cake or big Thanksgiving feast only to realize that you've completely run out of vanilla extract or that you underestimated the amount of vital wheat gluten you have in the house. The key to avoiding a mad dash to your nearest grocery store in the middle of preparing your celebration is to keep a well-stocked kitchen that is ready for any occasion. Here are some essentials you should keep handy.

## ACTIVE DRY YEAST

Yeast is a plantlike microorganism that serves as a catalyst to the fermentation process. This fermentation process is what makes dough rise and gives breads and dough made with yeast their airy texture. Baking and cooking with yeast requires a warm external temperature. In the summertime I usually keep my home around 78°F, but even this heat isn't enough to make yeast happy. The closer you can get to 85°F the better. There are a couple tricks to keeping your yeast warm enough to rise. The easiest one is to place the bowl with dough inside of it at the highest point in the kitchen, like on top of the refrigerator, where the temperature is warmer. Another great way to get your dough nice and warm is to place it near the oven or stove while you're cooking another dish. Or you can preheat your oven to 375°F, turn off the heat, then place your bowl inside, leaving the oven door open (do not do this with a plastic bowl). It usually takes yeast about 1 hour to rise in dough. I like to take this time to prepare the other dishes for my celebration feast (which also keeps the kitchen warm), or you can simply find a nice warm place for your dough to rise and take a nap.

## AGAVE NECTAR

Agave is most commonly known as the source of tequila. However, when you taste agave nectar, the last thing you'll think of is tequila (although it does make one great margarita). Agave nectar is a real sugar, as opposed to an artificial or nonnutritive sweetener. It has properties similar to many sugars with one important exception: its glycemic index is significantly lower. It can be found in nearly all conventional grocery stores and health food stores in the same aisle as the sugar and other baking supplies.

## CARDAMOM PODS

Cardamom comes in lightweight green or black pods that look pretty boring. But never judge a book by its cover. Those little pods are bursting with flavor, and the best part is you need not grind them, toast them, or roast them to get all that flavor out. Just drop them into recipes like Mulled Pomegranate Cider (page 210) and let the flavors slowly simmer out. The scent of cardamom is unique yet impossible to describe; however, the second the fragrance of cardamom hits your nose you'll be praising these little pods.

## CHIPOTLE PEPPERS IN ADOBO SAUCE

Chipotle peppers are smoked jalapeño peppers and adobo sauce is a rich sauce with tomatoes, garlic, vinegar, salt, and a litany of spices. Put the two together and you have a match made in smokey spice heaven. The heat of chipotle peppers is on par with jalapeños, although I find that the adobo sauce smoothes out the flavor a bit, turning down the heat a couple notches. Chipotle peppers in adobo sauce shine in recipes like Chipotle Black Bean Burgers (page 140), Huevos Rancheros (page 130), Flautas sin Pollo (page 134), and Tempeh Soft Tacos with Lime Crema (page 137).

## COCONUT MILK

For the longest time you could typically only find three types of coconut milk: light, sweetened, and unsweetened. No matter what the flavor, every variety came in a can. However, recently

So Delicious has come out with a coconut milk beverage that is sold in cartons right alongside soy and rice milk in the refrigerated section of the grocery store. This new coconut milk drink is perfect for pouring over cereal or even baking with instead of soy milk; however, it is much thinner than canned coconut milk and for this reason I never use it for stovetop cooking. Nothing beats the taste of rich, thick, and creamy canned coconut milk. Canned coconut milk is typically found on the ethnic food aisle at conventional and health food grocery stores.

## ENER-G EGG REPLACER

Ener-G Egg Replacer is a quick, easy, and simple option for replacing eggs in baked goods; 1½ teaspoons of Ener-G Egg Replacer whisked with 2 tablespoons warm water equals 1 egg. Ener-G Egg Replacer is also one of the most cost-effective ways to replace eggs in a recipe. One box has over 113 servings in it. It took me three and a half years to finish my first box of Ener-G Egg Replacer.

## FIVE-SPICE POWDER

My first trip to find five-spice powder took me over twenty minutes in the grocery store. If you're reading this section, then you will have the distinct advantage of learning from my mistake and making a beeline to the five-spice powder no matter what store you're in. Five-spice powder is not always in the spice aisle, although this is where you should look first. It is typically hiding on the Asian or ethnic food aisle and might be labeled "Chinese Five-Spice Powder." As the name implies, it is a blend of five aromatic spices that is a perfect mix of sweet, spicy, pungent, sour, and bitter. Although the recipe changes slightly from brand to brand, the typical spice blend will include ground cinnamon, ginger, star anise, cloves, and cassia buds.

## GARAM MASALA

*Garam masala* literally means "hot mixture"—however, the name can be a little bit misleading. Garam masala isn't hot as in spicy but is more of an intense burst of flavor. When cooking Southeast Asian and Indian food, I can't help but throw in a few

pinches of garam masala. It gives any dish an instant complexity that makes it seem like you've been slaving away in the kitchen all day when, in reality, you've barely spent 10 minutes at the stove. A little garam masala goes a long way. Try tasting the Tamarind Chutney (page 33) with and without garam masala and you'll see what a profound difference just ¼ teaspoon of this powerful spice mixture makes.

### GINGER BEER

With just one small sip of each you can easily tell the difference between ginger ale and ginger beer. Although the name has "beer" in it, like root beer, ginger beer is nonalcoholic. It carries with it the strong bite of ginger that is missing in ginger ale. You'll know you've found the perfect ginger beer if you look at the bottom of the bottle and see little flecks of ginger waiting for you. To make sure you get a consistent amount of ginger in each sip, it's helpful to store ginger beer on its side. Ginger beer can be found in most health food stores on the same aisle as other natural sodas. If you're looking for ginger beer in a conventional grocery store, try the ethnic food aisle near the Jamaican spices.

### GROUND ANCHO CHILE

Ground ancho chile can be hard to find but is well worth the hunt. I searched high and low through several conventional grocery stores and health food stores, but my search finally ended at an international food market where I was able to get a quarter pound of ground ancho chiles for only $1.50! I highly recommend seeking out an international food market in your area and perusing the spice aisle—you'll see more spices, herbs, and seasonings than you could ever imagine, usually all at a great price.

If you simply can't find ground ancho chiles in your area, you can make your own by pulsing dried ancho chiles in a food processor until they are ground down to a fine powder.

### JAMAICAN CURRY POWDER

Curry has become a catch-all word for any spice blend with coriander, turmeric, cumin, fenugreek, and dried red chile peppers in it. However, there are several different types of curry out there, all with different mixes of seasonings, spices, and herbs. Jamaican curry is a made of a blend of turmeric, coriander, fenugreek, salt, cumin, allspice, pepper, and garlic. Depending on the heat level of the curry, it can also have a little cayenne or ground red pepper flakes. You can typically find Jamaican curry in original and hot varieties in the ethnic food aisle of your grocery store. I highly recommend the hot variety. Don't be scared off by the heat; it is a mild heat that adds just the right amount of kick to dishes like Jamaican Curried Pumpkin Soup (page 206).

## KELP GRANULES

Kelp granules are kelp powder's big bad brother. The key difference between the two is flavor intensity. You can sprinkle a little kelp powder here or there without tasting much more than salt, but try sprinkling a few kelp granules on your midday snack and you will, without a doubt, get a nice fishy taste. Don't let this intensity of flavor scare you off. Kelp granules go perfectly in dishes like Fish and Chips (page 104) or Tempeh Cakes with Spicy Remoulade (page 34).

## KELP POWDER

Kelp provides a mild "fishy" taste to dishes like Fish and Chips (page 104) without being overpowering. What I love about kelp powder is that the flavor is mild enough for you to add just a pinch or two to a dish to give it a mildly salty taste without being too fishy. Unlike salt, kelp is naturally high in iodine and is often used as a nutritional supplement. You can find kelp powder in most health food stores either in the spice aisle or near the supplements.

## LIQUID SMOKE

Liquid smoke adds the distinct taste of outdoor grilling to indoor cooking. In vegan foods it adds a "meaty" flavor without being overpowering. In this book it is most often used when flavoring textured vegetable protein and gives that hickory, outdoor, smokey flavor to dishes like Southern-Style Greens (page 177), where pork or smoked turkey is traditionally used to the flavor the greens. You can find liquid smoke in most grocery stores, in the condiment aisle near the steak sauce.

## LOBSTER MUSHROOMS

Lobster mushrooms aren't mushrooms at all but are actually a parasite that grows on mushrooms. This parasite is what gives lobster mushrooms their distinctive red-orange lobster color. Not only do these bright-colored fungi look like lobster, but they have a light lobster/seafood taste that makes them the perfect stand-in for lobster and crawfish in recipes like Naw-Fish Étouffée (page 82). Lobster mushrooms can typically be found in larger grocery stores, specialty shops, and health food stores in the produce section. If you can't find fresh lobster mushrooms, then look for dried lobster mushrooms. They can be found in health food stores, specialty shops, and online. A 4-ounce package of dried lobster mushrooms equals 1 pound fresh. Simply pour warm water over the dried mushrooms and allow to sit for about 30 minutes, or until soft.

## NUTRITIONAL YEAST

Nutritional yeast is an inactive dry yeast prized for its "cheesy" taste. However it does more than just add a bit of cheese flavor when sprinkled on popcorn, soups, casseroles, gravies, salads, and steamed veggies. It also adds a creamy texture to the dishes it's added to, and just the right amount of sharpness to staple items like Chik'n Seitan (page 258). Not only is nutritional yeast delicious, it is also loaded with vitamins, minerals, and 8 grams of protein for every 1½ tablespoon serving.

Nutritional yeast is available in the bulk section of most health food stores. Look for the Red Star Brand, as it has the highest vitamin and mineral content.

## OYSTER MUSHROOMS

Oyster mushrooms are easy to spot. They smell like oysters, look like oysters, and taste like oysters. The oyster mushroom also contains natural statins and is currently being studied for its natural cholesterol lowering properties. These mushrooms are just an all-around powerhouse of a fungus and go perfectly in Oyster Po' Boys (page 88) and Fried Oysters with Cajun-Spiced Horseradish (page 86). Fresh oyster mushrooms can be found in health food stores and specialty shops. However, if you're not able to find fresh oyster mushrooms, try looking for dried mushrooms, which can also be found in specialty shops and health food stores, and online. Dried oyster mushrooms are less expensive than fresh and last longer. To rehydrate your mushrooms, simply place 4 ounces of dried mushrooms into a bowl with warm water and allow to sit until soft, about 30 minutes. This will yield approximately 1 pound oyster mushrooms.

## PANKO BREAD CRUMBS

Panko bread crumbs are Japanese-style bread crumbs that add the crunch you typically get from fried foods without all the fat. Panko bread crumbs are made from bread without crust and are lighter, flakier, and airier than traditional bread crumbs. They can usually be found in the same section of the grocery store as traditional bread crumbs, but if you don't see them there, head to the Asian foods aisle.

## POULTRY SEASONING

Don't be afraid of poultry seasoning. Just as steak sauce has no steak in it, poultry seasoning contains no poultry or any other animal by-products. What poultry seasoning does have is a familiar blend of spices that seems to always remind me of Thanksgiving for some reason. Typically, poultry seasoning is made up of ground sage, thyme, marjoram, rosemary, pepper, and sometimes a hint of nutmeg. It adds that something special to Spicy Seitan Burgers (page 44), Crispy Baked Tofu (page 120), and Corn Bread Stuffing (page 175).

## SILKEN TOFU

Silken tofu is a Japanese-style tofu that, as the name implies, has a softer, more delicate texture than Chinese-style tofu.

Silken tofu is packed two ways: in aseptic packs or in 14-ounce tubs. You can usually find aseptically packed silken tofu on the same aisle as the Asian foods in your grocery store, and the 14-ounce tubs of silken tofu in the refrigerated section near the firmer, Chinese-style tofu. In this book I use the aseptically packed version as it has a longer shelf life and doesn't have to be refrigerated. If you do choose to use the tub version, make sure it is plain silken tofu, as it now comes in vanilla, chocolate, and strawberry flavors.

Silken tofu comes in soft, firm, and extra-firm and works well when you want to create light and fluffy brunch favorites like the Papa Chorizo Frittata (page 132) or the Broccoli Frittata (page 116), or to give a velvety texture to desserts like Cheesecake (page 242) and Mexican Chocolate Mousse (page 114). It can also be used to make rich and luscious ice creams like Pumpkin Pie Ice Cream (page 186).

### SOBA NOODLES

Soba noodles are thin, hearty noodles traditionally made from a combination of buckwheat flour and whole wheat flour. Their origins are Japanese but they go fantastically in almost any Japanese, Chinese, or Thai dish. These noodles have an uncanny ability to grab every inch of sauce and flavor you throw at them. Any dish you make them with is sure to taste even better the next day once all the flavors have seeped into the noodles. Soba noodles are also one of the buried treasures of a conventional grocery store. They're usually always there but just a little hard to find. Canvas the ethnic or Asian food aisle and you'll usually find them somewhere near the middle or bottom, hiding out and just waiting to be discovered.

### SOFRITO

Sofrito is a cooking and seasoning base that is made by slowly simmering tomatoes, onions, garlic, green peppers, and cilantro. Making homemade sofrito takes at least 1½ hours. Why spend all that time laboring in the kitchen over a hot stove when there are plenty of store-bought varieties out there? You can find prepared sofrito in the ethnic or Latin-American foods aisle or your local grocery store.

## SPIKE SEASONING

Spike is an all-purpose seasoning that goes great on steamed vegetables, in popcorn, over pastas, in soups, or anywhere else you would traditionally use salt. It is extremely low in sodium yet still gives a nice salty taste. For the purposes of this book you'll only need the original-flavored Spike, the one with the red lid. Spike can be found on the same aisle as herbs and spices in your local grocery store or health food store.

## SRIRACHA

Sriracha is a Thai hot sauce made from chiles that are ground into a fine paste, mixed with just a hint of garlic, vinegar, sugar, and salt, and bottled for your eating pleasure. It is a bit thicker than traditional hot sauce or Tabasco sauce and has an "authentic taste"— you can tell that the ingredients are pure and simple. You can find sriracha in the Asian food aisle of your local grocery store or in your health food store.

## TAMARIND PASTE

Tamarind paste comes from the pulp of the tamarind fruit, a sweet and sour fruit that comes in little pods. Tamarind is used all around the world from India and Thailand to Nigeria and Tanzania. You can buy the pods whole and scrape out the pulp if you like, but why go through all that work when you can buy a jar of tamarind paste for just a few dollars? Tamarind paste can be found down the ethnic food aisle of your conventional grocery store. Because it is so widely used it can be found just about anywhere in the aisle, but is typically found near the Indian and Thai spices.

## TEMPEH

When it comes to tempeh, it isn't always love at first bite for everyone. However, once you get to know tempeh, you'll discover it's an incredibly versatile soy product, and, slowly but surely, you will find yourself gazing at it with love in your eyes. Tempeh is made from cultured and fermented soybeans. Once cultured and fermented, the soybeans are pressed into a perfect little tempeh cake ready for you to gobble up. The most commonly available tempeh in the United States comes in five different varieties: soy, three-grain, flax, garden veggie, and wild rice. My personal favorites are three-grain and wild rice. I highly recommend trying them all to get acquainted with your favorite tempeh flavor as well. Tempeh can be found at most conventional grocers and health food stores in the refrigerated section near the tofu.

### TEXTURED VEGETABLE PROTEIN (TVP)

Textured vegetable protein, or TVP, is made from defatted soy flour. It might not look like much, but once it is properly seasoned and cooked it takes on a texture similar to ground beef. Unlike store-bought faux ground beef, you can season TVP however you like. TVP is also an excellent source of protein—just ¼ cup of TVP contains 12 grams—and it's also a good source of iron. TVP can almost always be found in health food stores, either in the bulk section, the canned bean aisle, or the baked goods aisle near the alternative flours. It is also beginning to pop up in conventional grocery stores, so keep an eye out for it.

### VEGAN WHITE CHOCOLATE

Finding traditional semisweet vegan chocolate is fairly easy. Ghirardelli chocolate chips, one of the most popular brands, can be found in most conventional grocery stores and there are a variety of specialty brands that can be found in health food stores. However, vegan white chocolate is a lot harder to come by at conventional grocery stores but very easy to find at online vegan storefronts like Cosmo's Vegan Shoppe (www.cosmosveganshoppe.com) or Vegan Essentials (www.veganessentials.com). They tend to have a distant expiration date and they are super addictive straight out the bag so I highly recommend stocking up—otherwise, you might find that you eat your whole bag of chips before you get a chance to use them in a recipe.

## VEGAN WORCESTERSHIRE SAUCE

Traditional Worcestershire sauce contains anchovies, so it is a no-no for vegans and vegetarians. But have no fear, there are multiple brands of vegan Worcestershire sauce. You can usually find it near the liquid smoke in the condiments aisle of your local health food store. Depending on the brand, the label might say "vegetarian" or "vegan" but they are, indeed, both vegan.

## VEGETABLE STOCK

Don't fret if you head to your local grocery store and only see vegetable broth. The terms *vegetable stock* and *vegetable broth* are interchangeable. Although vegetable broth and vegetable stock are interchangeable, the type of stock or broth you use is important. I prefer to use a thin, light-colored, almost transparent vegetable stock in the majority of the recipes in this book. This type of stock adds a hint of flavor without being overpowering. A light vegetable stock is also great for cooking brown rice and quinoa instead of water to add a little extra flavor and seasoning.

I like to reserve the use of dark vegetable stock for rehydrating textured vegetable protein (TVP). Dark vegetable stock tends to have a richer, bolder flavor, and the richness helps bring out the flavor in the TVP. My favorite light vegetable stock is Swanson, and I've never met a dark vegetable stock I didn't like. The brand of dark vegetable stock varies by store. Most brands have a picture of the stock on the front of the package, so look out for a deep, brown stock.

## VITAL WHEAT GLUTEN

Whoever said being vegan is expensive never met a bulk bin of vital wheat gluten. One pound of vital wheat gluten can cost you as little as $2 to $3 when you buy it in bulk and $3 to $4 when you buy it prepackaged. Just ½ cup of vital wheat gluten is enough to produce a pound of Chik'n Seitan (page 258). Not only is vital wheat gluten inexpensive, but it is extremely high in protein—¼ cup has 23 grams of protein. Although vital wheat gluten is mostly used to make seitan in this book, it can also be used as a binder in dishes like North African Meatballs (page 220).

## WHITE PEPPER

When you see white pepper in recipes such as Tempeh Cakes with Spicy Remoulade (page 34), French Onion Dip (page 49), and Tempeh Reuben Sandwiches (page 106), do not, I repeat, do not substitute black pepper in its place. White pepper is black pepper's kinder, milder older sister. Black pepper is made from unripened peppercorns, while white pepper is made from mature peppercorns whose outer husk has been removed, producing a light peppery flavor that adds just the right kick without overpowering a dish. You can find white pepper on the spice aisle of your local grocery store.

## XANTHAN GUM

If you look on the back of almost any package of gum, natural toothpaste, ice pop, salad dressing, or commercial sauce, you will see xanthan gum listed in the ingredients. But what is it? The simple answer is that it's the glue that holds things together. Xanthan gum has become popular in home kitchens due to the increased interest in gluten-free cooking. Gluten typically acts as a binder in many baked goods, but when gluten is not present, xanthan gum steps in and takes its place. It is used in products like salad dressing to help the dressing stick to your salad green of choice and gives store-bought ice creams the same pleasant mouthfeel of homemade ice cream right out the churn.

I think xanthan gum is the best thing since sliced gluten-free bread. However, take caution: A little xanthan gum goes a very long way. Just ⅛ teaspoon too much and you can turn a dish from moist and smooth to sticky and pasty. So when experimenting with xanthan gum on your own, start with just a pinch at a time. Right at the point where you think you have an almost perfect consistency, stop and enjoy.

## The Crème de la Crème

Throughout this book I refer to a general "vegan cream" for recipes like Panfried Seitan with White Wine Herb Sauce (page 62) and Creamed Corn (page 125). There are several options out there in the world of vegan cream, and you have the freedom to use whatever kind suits your taste, sensitivities, and allergies.

Two of my favorite types of vegan cream are soy creamer and the gluten- and soy-free MimicCreme, which is made from nuts. Almost any type of vegan cream or creamer can be used for these recipes except coconut creamer, which will alter the flavor of your dish.

When using a soy-based creamer, make sure you always use a plain soy creamer, as anything else will adversely affect the flavor of your dish. Once you make the mistake of using hazelnut creamer in a creamed corn recipe instead of plain soy creamer, you'll be sure to never make it again.

MimicCreme, the gluten- and soy-free cream, comes in both sweetened and unsweetened varieties. I find that the sweetened version works better in the recipes in this book, and it's also great in your morning coffee or tea.

## Say Cheese!

When people tell me why they could never go vegan, overwhelmingly cheese is reason number one. I have to admit, as a vegetarian, cheese was one of the barriers that kept me from making the leap. But now, four years into going vegan I couldn't imagine eating cow's milk cheese, let alone craving it. What I do crave is vegan cheese. I love making my own homemade vegan cheese sauces for my Classic Macaroni and Cheeze (page 174), Game Day Nachos (page 52), and Loaded Potato Skins (page 48), but I've also fallen in love with several store-bought varieties. Here's a list of my favorites and where I like to use them.

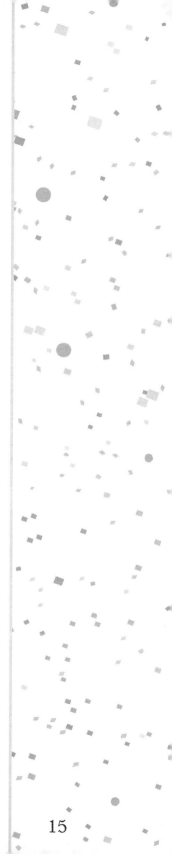

### CHEEZLY MOZZARELLA

There are currently at least seven brands of vegan mozzarella cheese on the market, but out of all the vegan cheese in the world Cheezly has won my heart. It melts to perfection and has a phenomenal light flavor. My Seitan Parmesan (page 58) and Rosemary and Chive Biscuits (page 118) wouldn't be the same without it.

### DAIYA VEGAN CHEESE

Daiya is, hands down, the closest thing to cow's milk cheese on the market today. It melts and stretches like cow's milk cheese, without the cruelty. As an added plus it's also soy free, gluten free, and nut free, so it's perfect for those with allergies and sensitivities. It comes in an Italian blend or mozzarella—ideal for pizzas, lasagnas, and other pasta dishes—as well as a cheddar flavor, which I love to make quesadillas with. My favorite recipe to use Daiya cheddar in is Roasted Red Pepper Corn Bread (page 229).

### GALAXY FOODS VEGAN PARMESAN

This vegan Parmesan-style cheese is probably one of the most true-to-taste Parmesans on the market. No one will ever know that you've switched out that yucky cow's milk version with this delicious vegan version. This is the only Parmesan that I will use to make my Seitan Parmesan (page 58) and Spinach Artichoke Dip (page 50).

### PARMA!

Parma is a raw Parmesan substitute made with just three simple ingredients: walnuts, nutritional yeast, and salt. Not only is it amazing sprinkled over Parmesan Roasted Asparagus (page 123), but it goes great on salads and sprinkled on popcorn.

I'm fortunate to live in a city where I have access to any type of vegan cheese I want, but if you don't happen to live in such a vegan-friendly city you can easily go online to great vegan retailers like Cosmo's Vegan Shoppe (www.cosmos

veganshoppe.com) and order any of the vegan cheeses mentioned above. You can also head to my blog, Vegan Guinea Pig (veganguineapig.blogspot.com), for updates and reviews on vegan cheese.

## Vegan Spirits

Once in a blue moon, usually at a cookout or holiday party, someone will ask me if I drink, since I'm vegan. My answer is always a resounding "Yes!" as evidenced by some of my favorite recipes in this book like Gingered Champagne Cocktail (page 42), Irish Cream Liqueur (page 111), Sweetheart Sangria (page 73), and Mulled Pomegranate Cider (page 210). As it turns out, I'm not the only one. There's even a popular movement of meet-ups called Vegan Drinks (www.vegan drinks.org) that happens at bars and restaurants all around the country every month.

Although most alcohol is vegan, there are some nonvegan offenders out there. It usually isn't the alcohol itself that isn't vegan but the way it's produced. Isinglass, made of fish bladders, is used to filter some beers and wines. Gelatin, egg whites/albumin, and seashells are also used as filters for wines, beers, and liquors. As a general rule all German beers are vegan, and most U.S. and Belgian beers are also vegan.

Barnivore (www.barnivore.com) is a great resource if you ever have a question about whether an alcoholic beverage is vegan. They were kind enough to help me find a local vegan stout beer for my Stout Beer Cupcakes with Whiskey Cream Cheeze Frosting (page 108), and they have a large database of vegan beers, wines, liquors, and liqueurs from national and international brands down to local breweries. Barnivore even has an iPhone app, so no matter where you go you can have the Barnivore database at your fingertips.

The blog Vegans Are From Mars also has an excellent vegan wine guide (vegans.frommars.org/wine) that breaks down wine from your typical supermarket brands all the way up to high-end specialty wines. They also have a handy wine pocket guide.

All in all, when you walk into your favorite liquor store you can rest assured that no animals were harmed in the making of your next hangover.

# Cooking Up the Basics

## DRIED BEANS

The cheapest things you will find in the grocery store are usually tucked away on the bottom shelf in large plastic bags or burlap sacks. They don't look sexy, and they're not super colorful— no bright blues, greens, or oranges here. But what they are is delicious little treats, jam-packed with fiber, protein, and essential vitamins and minerals. They're beans, of course!

For years I stayed away from dried beans. They looked like a pain to cook and definitely didn't fit into my hectic schedule. I was a die-hard canned bean girl. Just open the can, rinse, and serve. Then one day I came across a huge burlap sack of pinto beans with a price tag that read "$3 for 5 pounds." I was sold. I bought that bag of pinto beans two years ago and am still working my way through pound number three. It was, without a doubt, the best three dollars I've ever spent.

The key to preparing quick and easy dried beans at home is a pressure cooker and freezer bags. With the help of a pressure cooker you can have a pound of beans cooked to perfection, with no soaking needed, usually in no more than 30 minutes. A pound of beans goes a long way (depending on the type of bean, 1 pound dry beans can equal anywhere from 5 to 7 cups of cooked beans), so that's where the freezer bags come in. I like to portion out my beans into 2-cup batches and freeze them until I'm ready to use them. If you don't have any freezer bags lying around, old Vegan Mayonnaise jars, vegan sour cream tubs, and Mason jars also work great and usually hold around 2 cups of beans, depending on their volume.

Here's a basic guide to pressure cooking beans:

| BEANS (1 pound or 2 heaping cups, cooked with 8 cups water) | COOKING TIME (high pressure) |
|---|---|
| Black beans | 30 minutes |
| Cannellini beans | 35 minutes |
| Chickpeas/garbanzo beans | 50 minutes |
| Great Northern beans | 30 minutes |
| Navy beans | 30 minutes |
| Pinto beans | 30 minutes |
| Red beans/kidney beans | 30 minutes |
| Soybeans | 35 minutes |

## ALTERNATIVE FLOURS

### Arrowroot

Arrowroot is a pure starch and therefore a wonderful thickening agent. However, arrowroot has a low tolerance for temperature and tends to break down at high temperatures. You'll know immediately if you've cooked a sauce with arrowroot for too long because it will lose all its thickening properties and change to a thin jelly consistency. Although it is temperature sensitive, arrowroot is one of my favorite thickeners because it thickens very quickly and can be whisked directly into liquids without clumping up.

### Chickpea (Garbanzo Bean) Flour

As the name implies, chickpea flour is made from ground chickpeas (also known as garbanzo beans). Like chickpeas, chickpea flour is an excellent source of protein, boasting about 6 grams for every ¼ cup, and is also a good source of iron. Because of the recent boom in gluten-free products, chickpea flour is now showing up on the shelves of some conventional grocery stores, but is still most often found at health food stores.

### Masa Harina

Masa harina is made from corn that's been treated with a mixture of lime and water to help make important nutrients like niacin more digestible. It is then ground and made into masa. Masa harina is the dried form of masa. Masa is the base of many staples of Mexican food such as corn tortillas and tamales. I also like using masa harina as a binder in recipes like Cauliflower Latkes (page 192). You can find masa harina down the ethnic foods aisle of your local grocery store with the Mexican foods.

## Potato Starch

The name says it all. Potato starch is the extracted starch of the potato and is primarily used for thickening. You use potato starch much in the same way you would cornstarch; however, potato starch is able to tolerate much higher temperatures than cornstarch and therefore its holding properties last longer in high heat. Potato starch also tends to not clump the way that cornstarch does when you add it to sauces, soups, and stews, so you can whisk potato starch directly into a dish without mixing it with water first.

## Soy Flour

Soy flour is a high-protein flour made of dried, ground soybeans. Like its whole bean counterpart, soy flour is a good source of protein and iron. There are about 10 grams of protein in every ¼ cup of soy flour. Typically soy flour can be found in the baking aisle or bulk bins of many health food stores.

## Tapioca Starch

Tapioca starch and tapioca flour are synonymous. If you have either one, then you have the ingredient you need. Tapioca starch is a flour made from the cassava or yuca root and has a slightly sweet flavor. It is highly starchy and is therefore a great thickening agent.

## White Rice Flour

White rice flour is made from finely ground white rice. It has a lighter texture than all-purpose flour and gives dishes like Fried Oysters (page 86) a great crispy texture without overpowering the mushrooms. Although white rice flour can't typically be substituted for all-purpose flour in baking because of its lack of gluten, it replaces all-purpose flour perfectly in Southern Sweet Corn Bread (page 41) and Roasted Red Pepper

Corn Bread (page 229) to create gluten-free versions of these breads.

### Whole Wheat Pastry Flour

Whole wheat pastry flour is a whole-grain, whole wheat flour that has been finely milled to mimic the texture of refined wheat flour but retain all the nutrients of whole-grain wheat. Using whole wheat pastry flour in place of refined wheat flour gives the foods you cook more protein, fiber, and nutrients without sacrificing taste and texture. Do not substitute regular whole wheat flour for whole wheat pastry flour; the textures are very different and you will end up with a much denser product.

## GRAINS

### Brown Rice

Brown rice is a whole-grain, unbleached, unrefined rice that has a chewier texture than white rice. White rice is made by removing the husk, bran, and endosperm of the rice grain. This depletes several nutrients such as B complex vitamins, iron and other important minerals, and fiber. Brown rice is produced by only removing the husk of the rice, therefore maintaining its nutrient profile. Because brown rice has two extra layers (the bran and the endosperm), it takes longer to cook than white rice. To cook brown rice put 1 cup rice and 2 cups vegetable stock or water into a small pot. Bring to a boil, reduce the heat, and simmer, covered, for 50 minutes, being careful not to remove the lid. Once the rice has finished cooking, fluff with a fork and serve. This will yield about 3 cups of cooked rice.

### Jasmine Rice

Jasmine rice is a long-grain, fragrant rice with its origins in Thailand. Its flavorful aroma makes it a wonderful alternative to traditional white rice. To cook jasmine rice, put 1 cup jasmine rice and 1½ cups water in a small pot and bring to a boil. Reduce the heat, cover, and simmer for 20 minutes. Fluff with a fork and serve. This will yield 3 cups of cooked rice.

**Quick-Cooking Brown Rice**

Quick brown rice has all the benefits of brown rice without the fuss of a 50-minute cooking time. This rice is parboiled (which means it has been partially precooked) and is ready to eat in just 10 minutes. Oftentimes it is microwaveable and ready in 5 to 7 minutes, depending on the brand. Every brand has different instructions, so just follow the instructions on the box and enjoy!

**Quinoa**

Quinoa is a protein-packed "pseudograin" that has properties of both green leafy vegetables and cereal grains. Not only is it high in protein, but, like soy, its protein is complete, meaning its composition of amino acids is ideal for the human body. It is also high in fiber, iron, and other essential minerals. Quinoa is tremendously versatile and can be eaten like oatmeal for breakfast or like brown rice as a side dish.

When cooking quinoa it is important to first rinse it in water. The outer layer of quinoa is covered in saponins, which give the grain a bitter flavor. Although most commercial brands of quinoa are already prerinsed I always like to give it another quick rinse, just in case. To do so, pour the quinoa into a fine-mesh strainer and rinse, shaking off any additional water. To cook, bring 2 cups of water or vegetable stock to a boil and stir in 1 cup quinoa. Lower the heat and simmer, covered, until the liquid is absorbed, approximately 15 minutes. Fluff with a fork and serve. This will yield about 2 cups cooked quinoa.

# Gadgets and Gizmos

I'M ABSOLUTELY OBSESSED with kitchen gadgets and gizmos. I have so many that I had special units in my pantry made to store all of them and within weeks it was overflowing. Now I'm storing Crock-Pots, juicers, and mandolines everywhere from the kitchen table to the garage. There is, however, a method to my madness. Every gadget is in my life to simplify it and make the experience of cooking quick, easy, and enjoyable. Why spend hours slicing potatoes when I can do the same thing with a mandoline in seconds? Why get a cramp in my arm from mixing and kneading dough when a stand mixer can do all the work for me in a matter of minutes? You don't need to have the plethora of kitchen gadgets and gizmos that I have; however, the following items are essential for every kitchen— they will make your life easier and make cooking a pleasure.

## BAKING AND CASSEROLE DISHES

I am guilty of having one too many casserole dishes, cookie sheets, Pyrex dishes, pie plates, etc. You name it, I have it. I might have two. Or in the case of casserole dishes, three or four. Being a great cook doesn't require the arsenal of baking and casserole dishes that I hoard. You can get by quite nicely with these few basic items:

- Two 2-quart glass or ceramic baking dishes. One of them should be an 8-inch square pan.
- One 2-quart Dutch oven
- One 3-quart glass or ceramic baking dish
- Two 9-inch round cake pans
- One 9-inch springform pan

- Two baking or cookie sheets
- Two muffin or cupcake tins

## BLENDER

Blenders are excellent all-purpose puréeing and pulverizing machines, but not all blenders are created equal. I strongly recommend that you have a high-powered blender on hand. They are expensive, but they last a lifetime and can cut down your cooking time considerably.

High-powered blenders, such as the Vita-Mix, have up to a 2- or 3-horsepower motor that can pulverize even the toughest foods, such as avocado pits and macadamia nuts. These blenders even allow you to make warm soups and dips; the friction caused by the high-powered motor warms the food as it blends it. A high-powered blender is essential for making silky, creamy desserts like Raw Sweet Potato Pie (page 185). High-powered blenders also make quick and easy work of grinding nuts in dishes like Classic Macaroni and Cheeze (page 174), Cheeze Sauce (page 247), and Ranch Dip (page 251). If a high-powered blender is not in the budget right now, make sure you get the highest quality blender that you can afford.

An immersion blender is also helpful for puréeing soups and dishes like Creamed Corn (page 125), but not necessary.

## DEEP FRYER

A deep fryer might not be the healthiest addition to your kitchen arsenal, but it is one that I couldn't live without. When frying foods you can always use a large frying pan, and I give directions on how to use one instead of a deep fryer throughout the book. However, having a dedicated deep fryer is not only easier, but it cuts down on the mess and the hassle of filling, emptying, and cleaning a frying pan every the hassle you want to make Aloo Samosas (page 31) or Chorizo Empanadas (page 142). Look for a deep fryer with temperature controllers so you can easily set the oil to your desired temperature and simply wait for it to warm. Another advantage of a deep fryer versus a frying pan is the lid. No longer do you have to worry about hot oil splattering all over your kitchen (and all over you). Most deep fryers come with a breathable lid the keeps the oil in the fryer, where it belongs.

## DOUBLE BOILER

A double boiler is, essentially, two saucepans rolled into one. The double boiler has a little hole in it to feed water into the bottom saucepan and then allows you to slowly melt or cook the contents of the top saucepan without burning or charring. Typically, a double boiler is used to melt chocolate and make custards, and it also does a superb job of keeping melted chocolate at the perfect temperature while using it for sweet and spooky Halloween treats like Dirt and Worms Cupcakes (page 166) or Eyeball Cake Pops (page 164).

## FOOD PROCESSOR

I could not imagine life without my food processor, or should I say food processors. An army of three food processors, of varying sizes, keeps up with all the shredding, puréeing, and chopping that takes place in my little kitchen. However, the average kitchen only needs one great high-quality food processor of 4- to 6-cup capacity, and optionally, one mini food processor to mince fresh garlic and ginger. Don't forget to use all the parts that come along with your food processor. The S-blade tends to get a lot of use, but a lot of people forget about the shredding and slicing blade attachments that also come with nearly all food processors. The shredding blade of a food processor makes quick work of shredding potatoes, onions, sweet potatoes, and parsnips for dishes like Potato Latkes (page 190) and Sweet Potato and Parsnip Latkes (page 191).

## HANDHELD MIXER

The very first recipe I made as a child was for sugar cookies. My mother taught me that the key to the perfect cookie or moist delicious cake was creating a soft pillowy base of margarine and sugar. The process of creaming margarine and sugar is a near impossibility by hand, but a handheld mixer can get the job done in 30 seconds flat. Some handheld mixers also come with a whisk attachment that makes quick work of creating light, airy frostings, like Cream Cheeze Frosting (page 246).

## ICE CREAM MAKER

My mother used to churn homemade ice cream for my brother and me in the garage every summer. My brother and I only cared about the sweet, creamy end product, but my poor mother had to go through the laborious process of hand cranking the ice cream maker for nearly 30 minutes! Ice cream makers have come a long way since then, and making homemade ice cream is now a quick, easy, and fun experience for the entire family. A lightweight 2½-quart ice cream maker works perfectly to whip up Vanilla Bean Ice Cream (page 243) and Pumpkin Pie Ice Cream (page 186) in about 25 minutes. All you have to do is pour the ice cream mix into the freezer bowl, put the top on, and walk away—no hand churning required.

## LIME AND LEMON SQUEEZER

Fresh lime juice is what gives the Classic Margarita (page 145) its authentic Mexican flavor and brings out the right tartness and sweetness in desserts like Lime Sorbet with Mixed Berries and Chambord (page 69). However, staring down a stack of twenty limes can make the task of juicing them seem impossible. A handheld lime squeezer makes quick work of juicing limes and lemons. You simply cut the lime in half, place it in the chamber of the squeezer, and press down. The result is fresh lime juice without a trace of pulp.

There are specific squeezers for limes and lemons, but I highly recommend finding one that can be used to squeeze both. Combination squeezers typically run about $20, and single-purpose squeezers will usually run you anywhere from $10 to $15.

## MANDOLINE

A mandoline isn't essential for every kitchen, but it makes life so much easier. It produces uniform thin slices of potatoes for Au Gratin Potatoes (page 124) and perfectly proportioned

slices of onion for French Onion Dip (page 49). Depending on your style of mandoline, it can also julienne or crinkle-cut fruits and vegetables and cut potatoes for my all-time favorite, waffle fries. Some new models even have a dicing blade.

### PASTRY BAG

Pastry bags might seem like fancy-schmancy confectionary tools that only big-time chefs use, but they're actually super easy to use, and once you get the hang of it, they will make your life infinitely better. Both plastic and cloth pastry bags can be found nearly anywhere these days, from your basic home store to the grocery store. They are usually around $10 for a set of four, with different nozzle attachments to create an assortment of designs.

### PEPPER MILL

Nothing beats the taste of freshly ground pepper, which adds a bold and complex flavor to any dish. Although I like to use freshly ground pepper to finish a dish, I use preground when measuring pepper for recipes. Having both on hand will add variety to the dishes you prepare that you will immediately appreciate.

### SLOW COOKER/CROCK-POT

The terms *slow cooker* and *Crock-Pot* are virtually synonymous, so don't worry if you see the term *Crock-Pot* in a recipe and you have a slow cooker at home. They both do the same thing and do it well. As a single girl, the slow cooker is my best friend. After I drag myself into the house after a long day of school and work, the house is filled with the smell of a warm, homemade meal. Just throw all the ingredients in the pot, cover it, set the timer, and leave it alone until time's up.

### STAND MIXER

Handheld mixers are indispensable; however, stand mixers are the bigger, cooler, and more popular kids at the playground. Why? Because they can do things that a hand mixer only dreams about. A stand mixer comes with three attachments: a dough hook, a whisk, and a flat beater. My favorite application of the stand mixer is working with doughs that require yeast, like Sufganiyot (page 195) and Beignets (page 91). You can proof the yeast, make the dough, knead it with the dough hook, and let it rise all in the same bowl. This not only saves time, but cuts down the number of dishes you have to wash considerably. Stand mixers also make quick work of making frostings, cupcakes, cakes, and other confections all in one bowl with very little cleanup. The stand mixer is an exceptional addition to any kitchen; however, it is a pricey one—typically about four times as much as a handheld mixer. The price is largely a reflection of how simple it makes cooking. But don't fret if it's not in the budget just yet; all it takes is a little extra elbow grease and a hand mixer to get the same great results.

## STEAM BASKET

There's no need to get a big fancy dedicated steamer to steam your veggies; you can pick up a steam basket at any home store for about $4 and place it in any size pot or pan with a fitted lid. I recommend having a small and a large steaming basket. Use the small one for recipe likes Aloo Samosas (page 31) to steam up the Yukon Gold and sweet potatoes, and use the large steamer to steam Andouille Sausage (page 76) or other larger recipes.

## TOFUXPRESS

The TofuXpress is a handy little gadget that fits a 14-ounce to 1-pound block of tofu or a 10-ounce box of spinach. It presses out nearly all the water, leaving perfectly pressed tofu and squeezed spinach without the use of plates, weights, or towels. From one 10-ounce box of frozen and thawed spinach I was able to press out over ½ cup of liquid in just 2 minutes, giving the perfect taste and texture to my Spinach Artichoke Dip (page 50). Pressing the water out of your tofu leaves room for all the flavors you cook with to seep in.

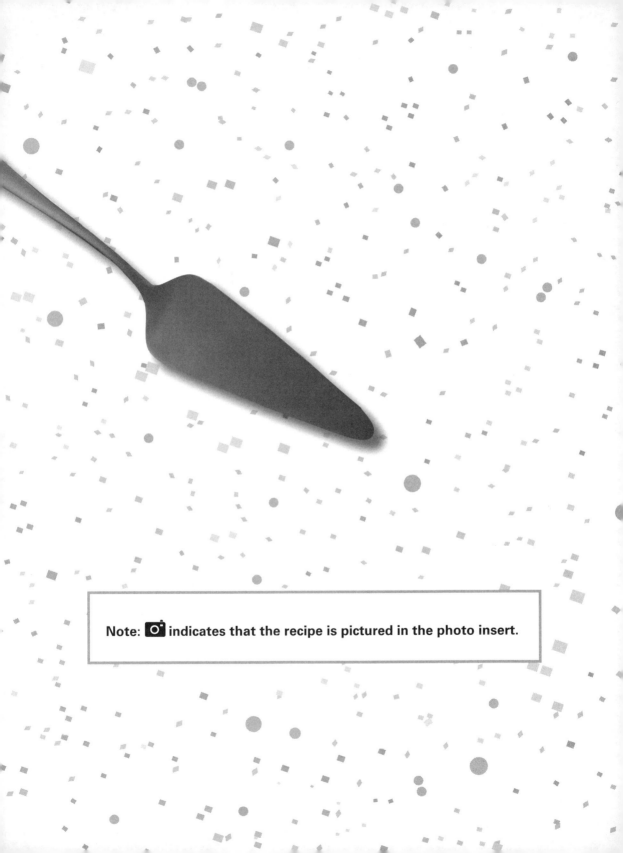

Note:  indicates that the recipe is pictured in the photo insert.

# ★ New Year's Eve ★

EVERY CULTURE HAS a unique and, oftentimes, tasty way of ringing in the New Year. There are as many traditional New Year's Eve foods as there are people on this Earth. In Spain, they ring in the New Year by eating twelve grapes to help ensure twelve happy and prosperous months ahead. In Greece, New Year's Day is celebrated with Vasilopita or St. Basil's cake. A silver or gold coin is baked inside the cake, and whoever finds the coin will have a year of good fortune. In the American South, black-eyed peas and cabbage are eaten at midnight to ensure a prosperous New Year.

Personally, the most important New Year's Eve tradition for me is to spend the evening with friends, family, and loved ones, so I like to create a spread of small bites and appetizers that everyone can enjoy and then follow it up the next day with a traditional Southern New Year's feast.

Aloo Samosas with Tamarind Chutney

Tempeh Cakes with Spicy Remoulade

Beer-Battered Green Beans

Sun-Dried Tomato Dip

Coconut Curry Peanut Noodles

Black-Eyed Peas

Cabbage

Southern Sweet Corn Bread

Gingered Champagne Cocktail

Chocolate Martini

# Aloo Samosas with Tamarind Chutney

MAKES 16 SAMOSAS

*Forget a big New Year's Eve party—these samosas are a little party in your mouth. The coriander and cayenne create a burst of flavor. Pair them with an unbelievably quick and easy-to-make Tamarind Chutney, and you have an instant hit.*

**PASTRY**

    2 cups unbleached all-purpose flour

    1 teaspoon fine sea salt

    ½ teaspoon baking powder

    ¼ cup shortening

    ½ cup cold water

**FILLING**

    1 to 2 Yukon Gold potatoes (about ½ pound), peeled and cut into 1-inch pieces

    1 small garnet sweet potato or yam (about ½ pound), peeled and cut into 1-inch pieces

    2½ teaspoons ground coriander

    ¾ teaspoon cayenne pepper

    1 teaspoon fresh lemon juice

    ½ teaspoon turmeric

    ½ teaspoon fine sea salt

    1 cup fresh or frozen and thawed peas

    Canola oil for frying

    1 recipe Tamarind Chutney (recipe follows)

**TO MAKE THE PASTRY:** Put the flour, salt, and baking powder into a food processor. Pulse twice. Add the shortening and pulse until the mixture resembles coarse cornmeal. While the processor is running, slowly add the cold water until a dough forms.

Transfer the dough to a bowl and let sit at room temperature for 30 minutes. Prepare the filling while the dough is resting.

**TO MAKE THE FILLING**: Steam the potatoes and yam until soft and tender, about 15 minutes. Transfer to a large bowl and mash, leaving some small chunks. Fold in the coriander, cayenne, lemon juice, turmeric, salt, and peas. Set aside.

These samosas can be cooked in a deep fryer or pan-fried on the stove. If using a deep fryer, preheat to 350°F.

On a floured surface, roll the dough into a rope about 12 inches long, then cut into 8 pieces. Roll each piece into a ball, then flatten into a patty. Roll each patty into a 6-inch circle, adding flour as necessary so it does not stick to the work surface. Cut each circle in half. Add 1 to 2 tablespoons of filling to each half circle, fold the pastry over, and pinch closed.

If pan-frying the samosas, heat about ½ inch of oil in a large frying pan over medium heat. To test the heat, sprinkle a small drop of water into the oil. Once the water begins to pop, the oil is ready.

Pan-fry or deep-fry the samosas in small batches until golden brown, 2 to 3 minutes, turning halfway through if not completely submerged. Drain on paper towels. Serve with chutney.

## Tamarind Chutney

**MAKES ½ CUP**

2 teaspoons tamarind paste

10 pitted dates

¾ teaspoon ground cumin

¼ teaspoon cayenne pepper

¼ teaspoon fine sea salt

¼ teaspoon garam masala

3 tablespoons water

Purée all the ingredients in a food processor until smooth. Cover and set aside until ready to use.

# Tempeh Cakes with Spicy Remoulade

**MAKES 9 TO 10 CAKES**

*Forget mock crab cakes and croquettes. These tempeh cakes stand on their own as a testament to what is great about vegan food—wonderful textures, phenomenal taste, and of course, inexpensive ingredients that are a snap to put together.*

One 8-ounce package tempeh, any variety

2 cups vegetable stock

¼ teaspoon kelp granules or powder

¼ cup chopped green bell pepper

¼ cup diced celery

¼ cup vegan mayonnaise

1 tablespoon vegan Worcestershire sauce

¼ cup diced white or yellow onion

2 tablespoons tapioca starch or arrowroot

1 teaspoon Old Bay Seasoning

¼ teaspoon cayenne pepper

¼ cup panko bread crumbs

2 tablespoons canola oil

1 recipe Spicy Remoulade (recipe follows)

Simmer the tempeh in the stock for 25 minutes. Discard any excess stock and set the tempeh aside to cool.

Grate the cooled tempeh and stir in the kelp, bell pepper, celery, mayonnaise, Worcestershire sauce, onion, tapioca starch, Old Bay Seasoning, cayenne, and panko. Roll a little less than ¼ cup of the tempeh mixture into a ball, and then flatten the ball. Repeat this with the rest of the tempeh mixture.

Heat the oil in a large skillet or griddle over medium-high heat and cook the cakes until golden brown and crispy on each side, about 2 minutes per side.

Serve with the Spicy Remoulade.

## Spicy Remoulade

**MAKES ⅔ CUP**

½ cup vegan mayonnaise

1 tablespoon whole-grain mustard

1½ teaspoons white wine vinegar

1½ teaspoons vegan Worcestershire sauce

1 garlic clove, minced

½ teaspoon paprika

1 teaspoon hot sauce

¼ teaspoon cayenne pepper

¼ teaspoon ground white pepper

Whisk together all the ingredients and chill, covered, for at least 1 hour.

# Beer-Battered Green Beans

**MAKES 6 TO 8 SERVINGS**

*Beer plus fried food always equals success. Your guests will love these green beans with Teriyaki Dip (page 252), Ranch Dip (page 251), or Dill Dip (page 249). If beer isn't your thing, no worries—you can substitute ginger ale for the beer.*

Canola oil for frying
1 cup beer
1 cup unbleached all-purpose flour
½ teaspoon fine sea salt
½ teaspoon paprika
½ teaspoon freshly ground black pepper
1 pound fresh green beans, ends trimmed

Preheat a deep fryer to 350°F or heat about ½ inch oil in a large frying pan over medium heat. To test the heat, sprinkle a small drop of water into the oil. Once the water begins to pop, the oil is ready.

Whisk the beer, flour, salt, paprika, and pepper until smooth.

Toss the green beans in the batter to coat. Fry in small batches until the beans are golden and crisp, 2 to 3 minutes. Remove from the oil with a slotted spoon or tongs (do not use plastic) and drain on paper towels.

# Sun-Dried Tomato Dip

*For some reason, at any and every party, I always gravitate toward the veggies and dip and end up hovering over it all night, leaving only to cut a rug, refresh my drink, and once again return to the dip. One taste of this dip and you'll understand my obsession.*

**MAKES 2 CUPS**

⅓ cup sun-dried tomatoes in oil, drained
1 cup vegan cream cheese
⅓ cup vegan sour cream
¼ cup vegan mayonnaise
¼ teaspoon cayenne pepper
¼ teaspoon onion powder
⅛ teaspoon garlic powder
⅛ teaspoon fine sea salt
Baby carrots, jicama sticks, and broccoli florets, for dipping

Put the tomatoes, cream cheese, sour cream, mayonnaise, cayenne, onion powder, garlic powder, and salt into a food processor and process until smooth. Serve with the vegetables.

# Coconut Curry Peanut Noodles

*Various Asian countries bring in the New Year with long noodles, representing a long and prosperous life. It is very important that you not break the noodles before you eat them, because it is bad luck. Throw etiquette to the wind and slurp down these noodles one a time, making sure not to break one—your future is depending on it.*

½ cup smooth peanut butter

1½ tablespoons fresh lime juice

1 tablespoon red curry paste

¼ cup vegetable stock

½ cup coconut milk

¼ cup loosely packed cilantro leaves, plus torn cilantro for garnish

¼ teaspoon fine sea salt (optional)

1 teaspoon maple syrup (optional)

One 12-ounce package spaghetti or soba noodles, prepared according to package directions

2 medium carrots, grated

¼ cup roasted peanuts, coarsely chopped

Put the peanut butter, lime juice, curry paste, stock, coconut milk, ¼ cup cilantro, salt, and maple syrup, if using, into a blender and blend until smooth.

Pour this mixture into a saucepan over medium-low heat and cook until the sauce is warmed through, stirring constantly. Add the pasta and grated carrots to the sauce and toss until the pasta is completely coated.

Serve warm, topped with the peanuts and torn cilantro.

# Black-Eyed Peas

*Eating black-eyed peas just after midnight on New Year's Eve or on New Year's Day is the only proper way to ring in the New Year in the South. Black-eyed peas represent luck and prosperity going into the New Year. Add a little Cabbage (page 40), which also represents money and prosperity, and Southern Sweet Corn Bread (page 41), and you would have to do a lot of things wrong to shake off all that good mojo!*

**MAKES 6 TO 8 SERVINGS**

1 tablespoon canola oil

¾ cup diced yellow or Vidalia onions

4 garlic cloves, minced

6 cups vegetable stock

1 teaspoon hickory liquid smoke

2 bay leaves

1 pound dried black-eyed peas

1 teaspoon sugar

Warm the oil in a medium stockpot over medium heat. Sauté the onions until translucent, 3 to 4 minutes. Add the garlic and sauté for an additional minute, making sure that the garlic does not burn. Add the stock, liquid smoke, bay leaves, peas, and sugar. Bring to a low boil, reduce the heat, cover, and simmer for 90 minutes or until the peas are tender. Remove the bay leaves before serving.

# Cabbage

**MAKES 4 TO 6 SERVINGS**

*Not only does cabbage represent the hope for money and prosperity throughout the New Year, but it's incredibly easy to make. Just chop, boil, and serve.*

1 cabbage (about 2 pounds), sliced thin

3 cups vegetable stock

1 bay leaf

Freshly ground black pepper to taste

Put all the ingredients into a large stockpot. Bring to a boil, reduce the heat, cover, and simmer for 30 minutes or until the cabbage is tender. Remove the bay leaf and serve.

# Southern Sweet Corn Bread

*In the South everything is a bit sweeter, and by a bit sweeter I mean that their iced tea (also known as sweet tea) has the consistency of maple syrup, and the corn bread is more cake than bread. If you're going to have a traditional Southern New Year's Eve celebration dinner then you might as well just give in and have a little Southern Sweet Corn Bread with it, too.*

**MAKES 6 TO 8 SERVINGS**

1 cup cornmeal

1 cup unbleached all-purpose flour or white rice flour

¼ cup sugar

4 teaspoons baking powder

¾ teaspoon fine sea salt

¼ cup canola oil

2 tablespoons white vinegar

1 cup plain rice milk

Preheat the oven to 425°F. Lightly oil a 2- to 2½-quart baking dish or a medium cast-iron skillet.

Mix the cornmeal, flour, sugar, baking powder, and salt in a medium bowl until thoroughly combined. Make a well in the center and add the oil, vinegar, and milk. Stir until there are no lumps left, then transfer to the prepared baking dish.

Bake for 20 minutes or until golden and a toothpick comes out clean. Serve warm.

# Gingered Champagne Cocktail

MAKES 8 COCKTAILS

*The champagne toast is, without a doubt, the most traditional way to welcome the New Year in the United States. Take a detour from the ordinary by spiking your sparkling wine or champagne with a little vodka and sweet ginger. The result is a sweet champagne cocktail with a bit of ginger bite. Happy New Year!*

¼ cup candied ginger
One 8-ounce bottle ginger beer
½ cup vodka
One 750 ml bottle sweet sparkling wine or champagne

Divide the candied ginger among 8 champagne glasses. Add 1 ounce ginger beer and 1 tablespoon vodka to each glass. Top off each glass with sparkling wine and serve.

# Chocolate Martini

MAKES 1 MARTINI

*Some people just can't call it a celebration unless chocolate is involved somewhere in it. With this chocolate martini you can feel like the party is complete.*

2 tablespoons chocolate liqueur
2 tablespoons vanilla-flavored vodka
1 tablespoon amaretto

Put all the ingredients in a cocktail shaker filled with ice. Shake and strain into a chilled martini glass.

# ★ Game Day Spread ★

ADMITTEDLY, I'M NOT a big football gal. I even made it through a year of cheerleading in high school without ever having to actually learn how the game was played. I might not be that into the game, but what I'm always into is food. While the sports fans are huddled in front of the big screen rooting for their favorite team and trash-talking the losers, I'm serving up quick, easy, and delicious snacks, sandwiches, and desserts that are guaranteed to keep a smile on everyone's face—even if your team is losing.

Spicy Seitan Burgers

French Onion Burgers

Sun-Dried Tomato Pinwheels

Loaded Potato Skins

French Onion Dip

Spinach Artichoke Dip

Seven-Layer Dip

Game Day Nachos

Roasted Five-Spice Nuts

Brownies

# Spicy Seitan Burgers

MAKES 4 BURGERS

*This is, without a doubt, my favorite burger ever and a must-have at every game party. However, Spicy Seitan Burgers are not for the faint of heart. Everything from the simmering broth to the seitan mix to the breading is drenched with spice. But, unlike most spicy foods that have sauce dripping everywhere, these sandwiches are mess free or, at the very least, less mess.*

**BROTH**

2 cups water

1 teaspoon fine sea salt

1 teaspoon onion powder

1 heaping teaspoon dried sage (not ground)

¼ cup nutritional yeast

1 tablespoon red pepper flakes

**SEITAN**

½ cup vital wheat gluten

¼ cup soy flour

2 teaspoons cayenne pepper

½ cup water

**BURGERS**

½ cup plain soy, rice, hemp, or oat milk

2 tablespoons Ener-G Egg Replacer

2 tablespoons sriracha

1 cup panko bread crumbs

½ teaspoon chili powder

¼ teaspoon poultry seasoning

¼ teaspoon fine sea salt

½ teaspoon paprika

Canola oil cooking spray

½ cup vegan mayonnaise

1 tablespoon chopped fresh dill

4 whole-grain wheat or spelt hamburger buns

4 leaves green leaf lettuce

**TO MAKE THE BROTH:** Combine the 2 cups of water and the salt, onion powder, sage, nutritional yeast, and red pepper flakes in a medium saucepan and bring to a boil.

**TO MAKE THE SEITAN:** Mix the vital wheat gluten, soy flour, cayenne, and the ½ cup of water in a small bowl. Transfer to a floured surface and knead into a thin ball of dough (about ¼ inch thick). Cut into 4 cutlets and drop them carefully into the hot broth.

Reduce the heat, cover, and simmer until all the broth has been absorbed (about 40 to 50 minutes), stirring every 10 minutes.

**TO MAKE THE BURGERS:** Preheat the oven to 350°F. Lightly grease a baking sheet with canola oil.

Whisk together the milk, egg replacer, and sriracha in a shallow bowl.

Mix the panko, chili powder, poultry seasoning, salt, and paprika in a separate shallow dish.

Dip the cooked seitan cutlets, one at a time, into the milk mixture, then coat with the panko mixture. Place the cutlets on the prepared baking sheet. Spray the tops of the cutlets with canola oil and bake for 25 to 30 minutes or until golden brown.

Mix the mayonnaise with the dill.

Spread the hamburger buns with the dill mayo, place 1 leaf of lettuce on the bottom half of each bun, then top with the seitan and the top bun.

# French Onion Burgers

**MAKES 4 BURGERS**

*Tired of the same old plain veggie burger that you will inevitably be stuck chomping on at cookouts and game-day parties year-round? I share in your frustration; after four years of veggie burgers and veggie dogs I was done with veggie burgers. Just adding a simple topping like French Onion Dip gives you a detour from the ordinary and turns a veggie burger into a cookout treasure.*

4 store-bought veggie burger patties, any variety

8 tablespoons French Onion Dip (page 49)

4 leaves red or green leaf lettuce

1 small tomato, sliced thin

4 hamburger buns, lightly toasted

Cook the veggie burger patties according to the package directions.

Arrange 1 cooked veggie burger patty, 1 leaf of lettuce, and a slice or two of tomato on the bottom half of each bun. Top each with 2 tablespoons of French Onion Dip and the top halves of the buns.

# Sun-Dried Tomato Pinwheels

*I acknowledge that "pinwheel" might not be the most masculine word, so my suggestion is don't even mention the name—just set them on the table and watch them disappear. Besides, guys aren't the only ones who watch football.*

**MAKES 6 TO 8 SERVINGS**

4 large flour tortillas, plain or flavored
1 recipe Sun-Dried Tomato Dip (page 37)
1⅓ cups watercress, torn
1 medium daikon radish (about 9 ounces), grated

Warm the tortillas in the microwave for 10 to 15 seconds to soften them up a bit.

Spread a thin layer of Sun-Dried Tomato Dip over each tortilla, then evenly top with the watercress and grated daikon. Roll the tortillas tightly, then cut into ½-inch slices with a serrated knife.

**MAKES 8 SERVINGS**

*Loaded potatoes are a sports bar favorite. Unfortunately, finding vegan loaded potato skins at a sports bar is pretty much an impossibility (unless you're like me and sneak in a couple of your own). Bring the sports bar to your house with these Loaded Potato Skins.*

4 large russet potatoes, scrubbed

9 tablespoons vegan sour cream

1 cup Cheeze Sauce (page 247)

2 tablespoons vegan bacon bits or roughly chopped store-bought vegan bacon strips

1 bunch chives, chopped

Fine sea salt to taste

Freshly ground black pepper to taste

### Cook's Tip

Although baking the potatoes is preferred, if you're short on time simply microwave your potatoes for about 10 minutes, then skip directly to scooping out the flesh and following the instructions from there.

Preheat the oven to 450°F. Line a baking sheet with nonstick foil.

Cut the potatoes in half lengthwise and place them cut side down on the prepared baking sheet. Bake for 30 to 35 minutes or until the potatoes are easily pierced with a sharp knife. Leave the oven on. Let the potatoes cool until enough to handle.

Scoop the potato flesh into a bowl, leaving ¼-inch-thick shells.

Mash the potato flesh with 1 tablespoon sour cream, and season with salt and pepper. Put the mashed potatoes back into the potato shells. Pour Cheeze Sauce over each potato evenly. Bake for an additional 5 minutes.

Remove the potatoes from the oven and top with the bacon bits, chives, and the remaining sour cream.

# French Onion Dip

*Who really knows what makes a French onion dip French? I use Vidalia onions fresh from my adopted home state of Georgia. However, Georgian onion dip just doesn't have the same ring to it as French onion dip. French or Georgian, it's a classic dip that is always a crowd-pleaser. Use any leftover dip to make French Onion Burgers (page 46).*

**MAKES 4 CUPS**

3 tablespoons canola oil

2 large Vidalia or yellow onions (about 1 pound), halved and sliced thin

3 garlic cloves, sliced thin

1½ cups vegan sour cream

1½ cups vegan mayonnaise

1 teaspoon fine sea salt

1 teaspoon vegan Worcestershire sauce

½ teaspoon ground white pepper

Freshly ground black pepper to taste

Ruffled potato chips or a mix of fresh vegetables

Warm the oil in a medium saucepan over medium heat. Add the onions and cook, stirring occasionally, for 20 minutes or until golden and beginning to caramelize. Add the garlic and cook for an additional 5 minutes. Remove from the heat and let cool for 5 minutes, then roughly chop.

Stir together the sour cream, mayonnaise, salt, Worcestershire sauce, and white and black pepper. Fold in the onion mixture. Cover and refrigerate for at least 1 hour or overnight. Serve with potato chips or fresh vegetables.

## Cook's Tip

Use a mandoline to make quick work of slicing perfectly uniform onions. This will also dramatically cut down on the inevitable "onion eye burn" you can get from slicing onions with a knife and ensure that your onions cook evenly.

# Spinach Artichoke Dip

MAKE 4 TO 6 SERVINGS

*Warm spinach artichoke dip is on the menu of every Americana restaurant and sports bar but is never, ever vegan. Does that mean it's time to pout and curse the world for not keeping a vegan spinach artichoke dip on the menu? No! It means it's time to make your own kick-ass version that will blow that omni-version out of the water.*

12 ounces soft silken tofu

½ cup canola oil

½ teaspoon onion powder

¼ cup nutritional yeast

1 teaspoon fine sea salt

2 garlic cloves, chopped

Freshly ground black pepper to taste

¼ cup vegan Parmesan

One 10-ounce package frozen chopped spinach, thawed and water pressed out

One 14-ounce can artichoke hearts, drained and chopped

Toasted pita bread, crostini, or tortilla chips

Preheat the oven to 375°F. Lightly grease a 2-quart casserole dish with oil.

Purée the tofu, oil, onion powder, nutritional yeast, salt, and garlic in a blender until smooth.

Transfer the tofu mixture to a medium bowl and stir in the pepper, Parmesan, spinach, and artichoke hearts. Transfer to the prepared casserole dish and bake for 20 minutes or until the dip begins to bubble and is warmed through. Serve with toasted pita, crostini, or tortilla chips.

# Seven-Layer Dip

There are so many great game day dips it's hard to pick a fa-vorite. It's like trying to pick your favorite child—impossible. Depending on the size of my party, I like to put out the Sun-Dried Tomato Dip (page 37), French Onion Dip (page 49), and Seven-Layer Dip (page 51), but if the crowd is small and I have to choose just one, this is my go-to. It's a bean dip, gua-camole, and salsa dip all in one, and always a crowd favorite.

1 cup vegan sour cream

¼ cup Taco Seasoning (page 253)

2 cups vegetarian refried beans

2 medium avocados, diced and mashed

2 cups salsa

1 cup shredded romaine, green leaf, or red leaf lettuce

½ cup chopped green onions

¼ cup sliced black olives

Stir together the sour cream and Taco Seasoning.

Layer all the ingredients in a serving dish in the following order (bottom to top): refried beans, sour cream mixture, avocado, salsa, lettuce, green onions, and olives.

**MAKES 6 TO 8 SERVINGS**

### Cook's Tip

**Make it an eight-layer dip by sprinkling 2 finely chopped jalapeño peppers on top of the olives for a little extra spice.**

# Game Day Nachos

*Two of the most personal and important choices you will ever make in your culinary life are what toppings you like on your pizza and on your nachos. For this reason I never pre-make a tray of nachos for a crowd. Instead I set up a buffet-style nacho bar, with all the toppings laid out, and keep the Cheeze Sauce warm in a fondue pot. Let your guests ladle the Cheeze Sauce over their chips and dress their nachos any way they want.*

1 medium Yukon Gold potato, peeled and diced

1 medium carrot, peeled and diced

½ cup diced white onion

1 garlic clove, chopped

1 cup water

½ cup cooked navy beans

¼ cup canola oil

¾ teaspoon fine sea salt

1 tablespoon fresh lemon juice

½ cup cashews

One 10-ounce can diced tomatoes with green chiles, drained

One 13-ounce bag tortilla chips

1½ cups cooked black beans

2 green onions, or 1 bunch chives, chopped

1 cup sliced green or black olives

½ cup fresh sliced jalapeño

2 cups shredded romaine lettuce

Combine the potato, carrot, onion, garlic, and water in a small saucepan over medium heat. Bring to a boil, lower the heat, and simmer, covered, for 10 minutes or until the vegetables are tender. The smaller you cut the vegetables, the less time it will take to cook them.

Put the navy beans, oil, salt, lemon juice, cashews, and cooked vegetable with the cooking water into a blender and process until completely smooth.

Transfer the sauce to a fondue pot or large mixing bowl and stir in the diced tomatoes with green chiles. Ladle the sauce over the tortilla chips and top with the black beans, green onions, olives, jalapeños, and lettuce, as desired.

# Roasted Five-Spice Nuts

MAKES 4 TO 6 SERVINGS

*These nuts are dangerous, but not in a bad way, I promise. Long after your guests have stuffed their bellies full on Spicy Seitan Burgers (page 44) and Loaded Potato Skins (page 48) their fingers will still, somehow, wander over to the bowl of Roasted Five-Spice Nuts. Before you know it, the whole bowl will be empty with only little crumbs of sugar and spice left at the bottom. The great thing about this recipe is it takes no more than 10 minutes to whip up, so you can put another warm bowl of Roasted Five-Spice Nuts out within minutes.*

1 cup raw almonds

1 cup raw cashews

1 cup raw pecans

1 tablespoon canola oil

2 tablespoons light brown sugar

2 teaspoons five-spice powder

Preheat the oven to 400°F. Line a baking sheet with parchment paper.

Toss the nuts, oil, sugar, and five-spice powder together in a bowl. Transfer the nuts to the baking sheet and spread in a single layer.

Bake for 6 to 7 minutes or until the nuts become fragrant. Serve warm or at room temperature.

# Brownies

These brownies are made with 100 percent whole-grain, whole wheat pastry flour, and with agave nectar instead of refined sugar. So when eating them, sit back, close your eyes, and pretend you're eating something really good for you.

**MAKES 12 BROWNIES**

¾ cup whole wheat pastry flour

½ cup unsweetened cocoa powder

⅔ cup agave nectar

1 teaspoon baking powder

¼ teaspoon fine sea salt

¼ cup canola oil

2 tablespoons plain soy, rice, almond, or oat milk

2 teaspoons vanilla extract

½ cup unsweetened applesauce

Preheat the oven to 350°F. Lightly oil a 1-quart baking dish.

Mix all the ingredients together in a bowl. Transfer to the prepared baking dish. Bake for 25 minutes or until a toothpick inserted in the center comes out clean.

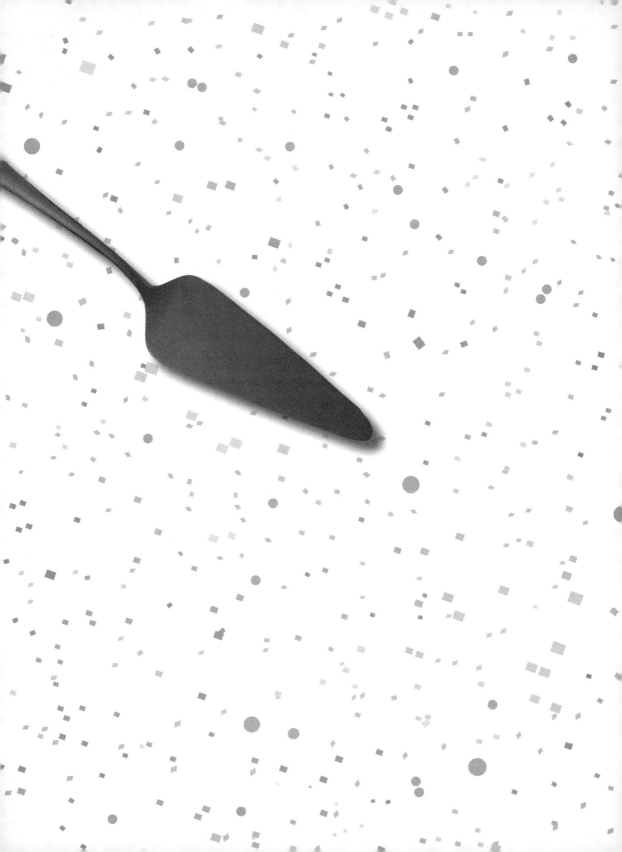

# ★ Valentine's Day ★

**E**VERY HOLIDAY HAS its own mascot, and Valentine's Day is no exception. A sweet little cherub with a bow and arrow is the maestro for this day of love. Now that Cupid's arrow has hit you, what are you to do? You've got your flowers, sweet and sappy card, and oversized teddy bear—but what's for dinner? You have a couple options this Valentine's Day: You can make reservations at a hoity-toity restaurant and share your evening with thirty-five other couples, or you can have a quiet, romantic evening at home, candles lit, with a little Kenny Loggins playing softly in the background and a quick and easy three-course Valentine's Day dinner.

Seitan Parmesan

Fusilli with Cabernet Sauce and Portobello Brisket

Pasta Puttanesca

Panfried Seitan with White Wine Herb Sauce

Spaghetti and Mock Meatballs

Ginger, Almond, and Fried Seitan Salad

Garlic Green Beans

Lime Sorbet with Mixed Berries and Chambord

Red Velvet Cupcakes

Bananas Foster

Sweetheart Sangria

# Seitan Parmesan

*Okay, fellas, if you're looking for the perfect meal to sweep your significant other off their feet, then this is the meal for you. And ladies, if you can't make Minute Rice without burning down half the kitchen, I promise you this recipe is easy and painless to work through. Pair with Garlic Green Beans (page 68) and you'll have a Valentine's Day dinner that will ensure you have a wonderful Valentine's night.*

1 cup panko bread crumbs

⅓ cup vegan Parmesan

1 teaspoon garlic powder

¼ teaspoon fine sea salt

¼ teaspoon ground black pepper

½ cup plain oat, rice, or soy milk

1½ tablespoons Ener-G Egg Replacer

1 recipe Chik'n Seitan (page 258), cut into 4 cutlets

Olive oil cooking spray

1 recipe Simple Tomato Sauce (recipe follows)

1 cup shredded meltable vegan mozzarella

Preheat the oven to 400°F. Line a baking sheet with nonstick foil and lightly oil.

Mix the panko, Parmesan, garlic powder, salt, and pepper in a shallow dish.

Whisk the milk and egg replacer in a separate shallow bowl.

Dip each cutlet into the milk mixture and then into panko mixture to completely coat.

Arrange the cutlets in a single layer on the prepared baking sheet and spray lightly with olive oil.

Bake for 15 minutes. While the seitan is baking, prepare the Simple Tomato Sauce (recipe follows).

Remove the seitan from the oven and cover each cutlet with 2 tablespoons of the tomato sauce and ¼ cup of the mozzarella.

Bake for an additional 5 minutes or until the cheese has melted. Depending on the type of vegan cheese you use, you might want to put the cutlets under the broiler for 1 minute to completely melt the cheese.

To serve, spoon 2 to 3 tablespoons of the tomato sauce onto each plate and place a cutlet on the sauce.

## ★ Simple Tomato Sauce

**MAKES 2 CUPS**

1 tablespoon extra-virgin olive oil

4 garlic cloves, minced

One 15-ounce can tomato sauce

1 tablespoon Italian seasoning

Warm the olive oil in a small saucepan, add the garlic, and sauté until fragrant, about 1 minute. Stir in the tomato sauce and Italian seasoning. Simmer, covered, over low heat for 10 minutes, stirring often.

### Cook's Tip

There are a few great vegan Parmesans on the market, but for this particular recipe, I like to use Galaxy Foods Parmesan Flavor Vegan Grated Topping. The light flavor melds perfectly with this dish.

# Fusilli with Cabernet Sauce and Portobello Brisket

**MAKES 6 SERVINGS**

*This sauce gives you a good reason to open up your favorite bottle of Cabernet Sauvignon and sip and stir, sip and stir. Cabernet is the star of this show, so make sure you use a good-quality wine. As a rule of thumb, only cook with wines that you actually like to drink.*

1 tablespoon extra-virgin olive oil

3 small shallots, sliced thin

4 garlic cloves, minced

¾ cup Cabernet Sauvignon

2 tablespoons agave nectar

2 teaspoons dried basil

1 teaspoon dried rosemary

½ teaspoon fine sea salt

¼ teaspoon red pepper flakes

1 cup vegetable stock

One 14-ounce can crushed tomatoes

One 6-ounce can tomato paste

One 16-ounce package fusilli

1 recipe Portobello Brisket (page 188), sliced thin

Warm the oil in a medium saucepan over medium heat. Add the shallots and sauté for 3 minutes. Add the garlic and sauté for an additional 30 seconds.

Add the Cabernet, agave nectar, basil, rosemary, salt, red pepper flakes, stock, crushed tomatoes, and tomato paste, stirring to combine. Bring to a low boil, reduce the heat, cover, and simmer for 20 minutes.

While the sauce is cooking, prepare the fusilli according to the package directions. Divide the pasta among serving plates and top with the Cabernet sauce and Portobello Brisket.

# Pasta Puttanesca

*Don't let the amount of garlic in this recipe scare you. Sautéing thinly sliced garlic gently in olive oil gives it an almost sweet taste, similar to that of roasted garlic. If your concern is the ever-unromantic garlic breath, don't worry—two garlics cancel each other out.*

**MAKES 4 SERVINGS**

2 tablespoons extra-virgin olive oil

8 garlic cloves, sliced thin

¾ teaspoon red pepper flakes

One 14-ounce can petite diced tomatoes, drained

One 14-ounce can crushed tomatoes

1 teaspoon balsamic vinegar

2 tablespoons capers

1 teaspoon fine sea salt

One 14-ounce package fettuccine or linguine, cooked according to the package directions

Warm the oil in a medium saucepan over medium heat. Add the garlic and sauté for 5 minutes or until tender. Stir often to ensure the garlic doesn't burn.

Add the red pepper flakes and cook an additional 30 seconds. Stir in the tomatoes, vinegar, capers, and salt. Cover, reduce the heat, and simmer for 10 minutes. Toss the pasta and sauce together. Serve immediately.

# Panfried Seitan with White Wine Herb Sauce

MAKES 4 SERVINGS

*After the seitan is made, this dish takes just minutes to put together. So, you can devote your time this Valentine's Day to cuddling up with the one you love and not slaving away in the kitchen for hours. When choosing a wine for the White Wine Herb Sauce, be sure to pick a good-quality wine that you actually enjoy drinking. A lot of the alcohol cooks out of the sauce, but what stays is the flavor. Pop open your favorite bottle, add a little to the sauce, and put the rest out on the table to sip with dinner.*

### PANFRIED SEITAN

Extra-virgin olive oil for panfrying

1 recipe Chik'n Seitan (page 258), cut into 4 cutlets

½ cup unbleached all-purpose flour

### WHITE WINE HERB SAUCE

1 small shallot, sliced thin

¼ teaspoon fine sea salt

2 garlic cloves, sliced thin

½ cup dry white wine

1 cup vegetable stock

2 tablespoons vegan cream

1 teaspoon potato starch

2 teaspoons minced fresh thyme

2 teaspoon minced fresh marjoram

Freshly ground black pepper to taste

**TO PREPARE THE SEITAN:** Pour in just enough oil to cover the bottom of a medium skillet and warm the oil over medium heat.

Dredge the seitan cutlets in the flour and fry until golden, 2 to 3 minutes on each side. Drain on paper towels.

**TO MAKE THE SAUCE**: Put the shallot and salt in the oil left in the skillet from the seitan. Cook over medium heat until softened, about 2 minutes. Add the garlic and sauté for an additional 30 seconds. Stir in the wine and stock. Bring the mixture to a simmer and cook for 5 minutes.

Whisk in the cream and potato starch. Bring back to a simmer and cook until the sauce has slightly thickened.

Remove the pan from the heat and stir in the thyme and marjoram. Season with the pepper.

Transfer the seitan cutlets to a serving dish. Spoon the sauce over the cutlets and serve.

# Spaghetti and Mock Meatballs

MAKES 4 TO 6 SERVINGS

*Remember that classic scene in* Lady and the Tramp *when the two dogs from different sides of the tracks are sharing a plate of spaghetti and meatballs and they accidentally kiss? Re-create that sweet moment with this version of spaghetti and mock meatballs.*

1 cup dark vegetable stock

1 teaspoon hickory liquid smoke

1 teaspoon vegan Worcestershire sauce

1 cup textured vegetable protein (TVP)

¾ cup unseasoned bread crumbs

1 tablespoon vital wheat gluten

2 tablespoons minced parsley

2 garlic cloves, minced

¼ cup plus 3 tablespoons ketchup

¼ teaspoon fine sea salt

¼ teaspoon ground black pepper

Canola oil or canola oil cooking spray

One 16-ounce package spaghetti, cooked according to the package directions

1 recipe Tomato Sauce (recipe follows)

Bring the stock, liquid smoke, and Worcestershire sauce to a boil in a small pot. Remove from the heat, stir in the TVP, and let sit for 5 minutes.

Mix the bread crumbs, reconstituted TVP, vital wheat gluten, parsley, garlic, ketchup, salt, and pepper. Bring the mixture together with your hands. Form rounded tablespoons of the mixture into balls and place them on a large plate or baking dish. Refrigerate for about 1 hour.

These meatballs can be either panfried or baked. To panfry the meatballs, pour just enough canola oil into a medium skillet to fill the bottom of the pan. Warm the oil over medium heat, then add the meatballs. Cook on all sides until browned, about 10 minutes. Drain on paper towels.

To bake the meatballs, preheat the oven to 350°F. Line a baking sheet with parchment paper. Arrange the meatballs on the baking sheet in a single layer and spray with canola oil. Bake until browned and firm, 20 to 25 minutes, flipping them halfway through and spraying with canola oil.

Portion out the spaghetti among serving plates, then top with the Tomato Sauce and meatballs. Serve warm.

## ⭐ Tomato Sauce

**MAKES 3½ CUPS**

One 28-ounce can of whole tomatoes
⅓ cup tomato paste
1 tablespoon extra-virgin olive oil
½ cup diced white onion
5 garlic cloves, 3 minced and 2 chopped
¼ teaspoon red pepper flakes
1 teaspoon Italian seasoning
½ teaspoon fine sea salt
Freshly ground black pepper to taste
3 tablespoons dried basil

Purée the tomatoes and tomato paste in a blender.

Warm the oil in a medium saucepan over medium heat. Add the onion and sauté for 2 minutes. Add the garlic and red pepper flakes and cook for an additional minute. Stir in the puréed tomatoes, Italian seasoning, and salt and season with pepper. Simmer for 10 minutes. Remove from the heat and stir in the basil.

# Ginger, Almond, and Fried Seitan Salad

MAKES 2 LARGE OR 4 SMALL
SERVINGS

*This Valentine's Day salad is no wimpy side dish. It is as strong as your love (or lust . . . I'm not judging) and will leave you full and satisfied.*

### DRESSING

2 tablespoons molasses

2 tablespoons agave nectar

¼ cup extra-virgin olive oil

¼ cup apple cider vinegar

1 tablespoon minced fresh ginger

¼ teaspoon fine sea salt

¼ teaspoon hot sauce

### SEITAN

½ cup unbleached all-purpose flour

¼ teaspoon garlic powder

⅛ teaspoon ground black pepper

¼ cup plain oat, rice, or soy milk

1 tablespoon agave nectar

1 recipe Chik'n Seitan (page 258), cut into strips

Canola oil for frying

### SALAD

4 cups thinly sliced mixed greens

1 cup shredded carrots

¼ cup chopped green onions

½ cup raw or blanched almonds, sliced

**TO MAKE THE DRESSING**: Whisk together all the dressing ingredients, cover, and allow the flavors to blend in the refrigerator while preparing the rest of the dish.

**TO MAKE THE SEITAN**: Preheat a deep fryer to 375°F or heat about ½ inch of oil in a large frying pan over medium heat. To test the heat, sprinkle a small drop of water into the oil. Once the water begins to pop, the oil is ready.

Mix the flour, garlic powder, and pepper in a shallow dish. Mix the milk and agave nectar in a separate shallow dish. Dip each strip of seitan into the milk mixture, then into the flour mixture. Fry until golden brown, about 2 minutes. Drain on paper towels.

**TO MAKE THE SALAD**: Combine the greens, carrots, and green onions in a large serving bowl and toss with the dressing. Top with the seitan and sliced almonds. Serve immediately.

# Garlic Green Beans

*I know it might sound odd, but I'm in love with green beans. I even named my childhood blanket Green Bean. My Valentine's Day gift to you is to share my favorite vegetable with you in this quick and easy side dish. Feel free to substitute fresh baby spinach for haricots verts in this dish. Follow the instructions, using 1 pound of fresh uncooked baby spinach, upping the olive oil to 3 tablespoons, and forgoing the almonds.*

2 tablespoons extra-virgin olive oil

1 small shallot, sliced thin

3 garlic cloves, sliced thin

10 ounces haricots verts or green beans, steamed

¼ cup raw or blanched almonds, slivered (optional)

Fine sea salt to taste

Freshly ground black pepper to taste

## Cook's Tip

Haricots verts are simply long French green beans. *Haricot vert* literally translates to "green bean" in French. If you can't find haricots verts, feel free to substitute your standard green beans in their place.

Warm the olive oil in a medium skillet over medium heat. Add the shallot and garlic and sauté for 3 to 4 minutes or until softened. Add the haricots verts and sauté for 2 minutes more.

If using almonds, add the almonds and cook an additional minute. Remove the from heat. Season with salt and pepper and serve.

# Lime Sorbet with Mixed Berries and Cha

*A little Food Science 101: Adding just a touch of vodka to your sorbet will keep it creamy and light and prevent hard crystals from forming when you freeze it. So whether you're serving it straight out of the mixer or from an airtight container in the freezer, you'll still have the same smooth, creamy consistency.*

3 cups mixed fresh berries (raspberries, blueberries, and blackberries)

⅔ cup Chambord

1¾ cups sugar

1 tablespoon lime zest

2 cups water

1 cup fresh lime juice (about 8 large limes)

2 teaspoons vodka, optional

Gently mix the berries and Chambord in a medium bowl. Cover and chill while you prepare the sorbet.

Bring the sugar, lime zest, and water to a low boil in a medium saucepan, stirring constantly until the sugar dissolves. Remove from the heat and stir in the lime juice. Cool to room temperature then stir in the vodka, if using. Transfer to a 1-quart container with an airtight lid and refrigerate for at least 1 hour or until very cold.

Put the mixture into an ice cream maker and freeze according to manufacturer's directions, about 30 minutes. Serve immediately or freeze in an airtight container for up to 3 days. The longer the sorbet freezes, the firmer it will become.

Scoop the sorbet into servings bowls. Spoon the Chambord and berry mixture over the sorbet and serve.

# Red Velvet Cupcakes

*Somehow I made it through almost twenty years of life without trying my first red velvet cake. Within one week of moving to the South I had my first slice, and I've never looked back. These cupcakes are perfect for all Valentine's Day celebrations. When your child's teacher requests that you provide the treats for the class Valentine's Day party, this is an ideal go-to recipe. It is also the perfect end to a Valentine's Day dinner with your lady or beau.*

2½ cups unbleached all-purpose flour

1 teaspoon baking soda

1½ teaspoons baking powder

1 teaspoon fine sea salt

2 tablespoons unsweetened cocoa powder

1½ cups sugar

1 cup nonhydrogenated margarine, softened

½ cup shortening

1 cup plain soy, oat, or rice milk

¼ cup unsweetened applesauce

1 tablespoon plus 2 teaspoons white vinegar

1 teaspoon red food coloring, or 2 teaspoons beet juice

1 teaspoon vanilla extract

1 recipe Cream Cheeze Frosting (page 246)

Preheat the oven to 350°F. Line two 12-cup cupcake tins with paper baking cups.

Sift the flour, baking soda, baking powder, salt, and cocoa powder into a medium bowl.

Cream the sugar, margarine, and shortening in a separate large bowl with an electric mixer on high speed. Incorporate the milk, beating well. Add the applesauce, vinegar, food coloring, and vanilla, and beat well.

Add the flour mixture a heaping ½ cup at a time, beating well after each addition.

Divide the batter among the cupcake tins, filling each cup approximately three-quarters full. Bake one pan at a time until a toothpick comes out clean, about 20 minutes.

Cool the cupcakes completely before frosting with the Cream Cheeze Frosting.

## Cook's Tip

When using beet juice as a food coloring, I call for double the amount one would normally use, as the color is a bit lighter than traditional concentrated food colorings or their vegan alternatives.

# Bananas Foster

*Maybe I'm just strange, but I think that a flambéed dessert is one of the most romantic ends to a meal. Of course, all the romance wears off if you manage to burn yourself, so safety first. When preparing to flambé, make sure any long hair is pulled back, use a long wooden fireplace match so you can keep your distance from the fire, and remember—if the flame gets a little too high for your comfort level, simply put a lid over the skillet and the fire will die out quickly.*

¼ cup nonhydrogenated margarine

½ cup loosely packed light brown sugar

⅛ teaspoon ground cinnamon

3 large ripe bananas, halved lengthwise and widthwise

¼ cup dark or spiced rum

1 recipe Vanilla Bean Ice Cream (page 243)

Melt the margarine in a medium skillet over medium heat. Add the sugar and cinnamon and stir until combined. Add the bananas and cook until they are soft but not mushy and begin to turn a shiny gold color, about 2 minutes on each side.

Remove from the heat and add the rum. Wave a lit match over the pan until the rum lights. Lightly shake the pan to distribute the flame. The flame should subside on its own in about 30 seconds—if it does not, simply cover the skillet with a lid.

Divide the ice cream among serving bowls (about 2 scoops per bowl) and top with the bananas and the sauce from the pan. Serve immediately.

*This is sangria is for lovers only—lovers of vodka that is. It has the sweet, light, fruity taste of traditional sangria, but it is infused with a little vodka to take you places traditional sangria never could.*

1 cup raspberries

1½ cups sliced and peeled peaches (about 2 large peaches)

1½ cups sliced white or yellow nectarines (about 2 large nectarines)

2 tablespoons agave nectar

6 tablespoons Campari

1 cup sweet vermouth

1 cup vodka

Two 750 ml bottles chilled sparkling Moscato wine

Put all the ingredients in a large pitcher and stir to combine. Serve chilled or over ice.

**Cook's Tip:**

If nectarines aren't available, you can double up on the peaches or add another fruit of your choosing. Sliced mango, papaya, or red pears make great alternatives.

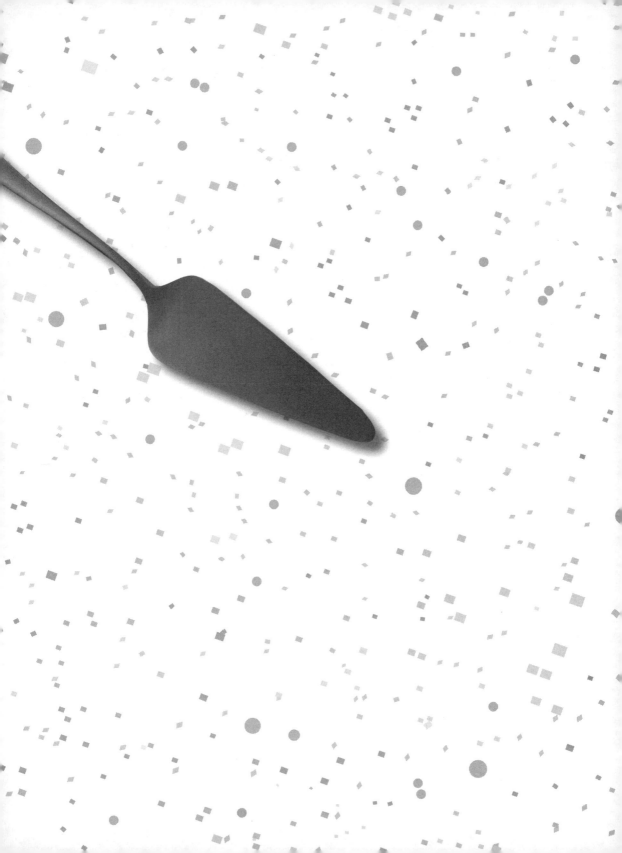

# ★ Mardi Gras ★

ALL AROUND THE world, the day before Ash Wednesday is celebrated with parades, drinking, dancing, and eating all the greasiest fried foods you can possibly stuff down. Whether you call it Carnival, Fat Tuesday, or its most popular name in the States, Mardi Gras, the Tuesday before Lent is spent doing all the things you won't be able to do for the next forty days and forty nights. There isn't a city in the United States that does Mardi Gras better than New Orleans. Mardi Gras is celebrated for a full two weeks before Ash Wednesday, but the celebration really kicks up in the final weekend and days leading up to Fat Tuesday. There are parades, masquerade balls, loads of colorful beads flying through the air, and a lot of flashing (and I'm not talking about lights).

New Orleans is known for its French Creole food, Cajun spices, and of course lots of fried pastries and desserts. Bring a little taste of New Orleans to your house this Mardi Gras season with this festive menu that is a sample of the best of New Orleans cuisine.

Andouille Sausage

Jambalaya

Gumbo

Naw-Fish Étouffée

Lobster and Cheese Grits

Fried Oysters with Cajun-Spiced Horseradish

Oyster Po' Boys

Bourbon Street Tofu

Dirty Rice

Beignets

Baked Beignets with Chocolate Almond Sauce

King Cake

Hurricane

# Andouille Sausage

MAKES 4 SAUSAGES

*Andouille is a spicy, smokey sausage with French origins that has become a favorite in Cajun cooking. It is most often used in famous New Orleans classics like Jambalaya (page 78) and Gumbo (page 80), but I also love it sliced thin and panfried as a breakfast sausage or piled high inside a hoagie roll. The heat on this sausage is mild, so feel free to add a teaspoon of cayenne pepper for more spice.*

1 cup vital wheat gluten

½ cup soy flour

2 tablespoons nutritional yeast

1½ teaspoons paprika

⅛ teaspoon ground black pepper

1 teaspoon red pepper flakes

¼ teaspoon ground allspice

1 teaspoon dried thyme

½ cup water

4 garlic cloves, minced

1 tablespoon Bragg Liquid Aminos

1 tablespoon tahini

¼ cup ketchup

2 tablespoons extra-virgin olive oil

2 tablespoons vegan Worcestershire sauce

¾ teaspoon hickory liquid smoke

Mix the vital wheat gluten, soy flour, nutritional yeast, paprika, black pepper, red pepper flakes, allspice, and thyme in a medium bowl.

Whisk together the water, garlic, liquid aminos, tahini, ketchup, olive oil, Worcestershire sauce, and liquid smoke in a small bowl. Add this wet mixture to the flour mixture and stir well, forming a dough.

Divide the dough into 4 balls, then roll each ball into a 6-inch log. Wrap each log tightly in aluminum foil (if you don't wrap them tight enough, they will burst out). Twist the ends of the foil to seal.

Place the sausages into a steamer and steam for 40 minutes. Remove from the steamer and allow to cool. Remove the foil and refrigerate until ready to eat.

# Jambalaya

**MAKES 6 TO 8 SERVINGS**

*Jambalaya is one of the hallmarks of French Creole cooking in Louisiana and one of my favorite dishes from the region. Most of the components in this Jambalaya can be made ahead of time. I highly recommend making the Chik'n Seitan (page 258) and Andouille Sausage (page 76) a day or two ahead of time so on Fat Tuesday all you have to do is sauté and simmer your way to a perfect jambalaya.*

10 tablespoons canola oil

1 recipe Chik'n Seitan (page 258), shaped into cutlets

2 links Andouille Sausage (page 76), cut into ¼-inch slices

½ cup diced yellow or white onion

½ green bell pepper, diced

½ red bell pepper, diced

½ teaspoon red pepper flakes

2 tablespoons unbleached all-purpose flour

One 14-ounce can petite diced tomatoes, with juices

1½ cups vegetable stock

2 bay leaves

1 teaspoon ground cumin

1 teaspoon chili powder

½ teaspoon poultry seasoning

1 teaspoon vegan Worcestershire sauce

Fine sea salt to taste

Freshly ground black pepper to taste

2 cups cooked white or brown rice

Warm 4 tablespoons of the oil in a large skillet over medium heat. Add the seitan and sauté until lightly browned on all sides, about 3 minutes. Add 3 tablespoons of the oil to the pan along with the sliced sausage and cook for an additional 3 minutes. Add the remaining 3 tablespoons of oil, along with the onion, green and red bell pepper, and red pepper flakes, and cook for 5 minutes.

Sprinkle the flour over the mixture and stir to coat. Stir in the tomatoes, stock, bay leaves, cumin, chili powder, poultry seasoning, and Worcestershire sauce. Cook for 5 minutes, then remove the bay leaves and season with salt and pepper.

Divide the rice among serving plates or bowls, then top with the Jambalaya.

# Gumbo

MAKES 4 TO 6 SERVINGS

*Gumbo is the essence of true Louisiana cooking. The key to every good gumbo is the roux. Roux might sound like a mystical being, but in fact it's simply a slowly cooked mixture of margarine and flour. The key to a good roux is patience. It requires about 20 minutes of constant stirring over medium-low heat to get it just right. You'll know you have the perfect roux when your mixture has reached a deep caramel color.*

*I apologize ahead of time to all you okra fans. Okra and I have been mortal enemies since my childhood, and therefore I've omitted it from this gumbo. If you simply can't imagine gumbo without okra, add about 1 cup of sliced fresh or frozen okra when you add the diced tomatoes.*

3 tablespoons canola oil

1 recipe Chik'n Seitan (page 258), shaped into cutlets and coarsely chopped

2 links Andouille Sausage (page 76), sliced into ¼-inch medallions

4 tablespoons nonhydrogenated margarine

¼ cup unbleached all-purpose flour

½ cup diced yellow or white onion

4 garlic cloves, minced

½ green bell pepper, diced

1 celery rib, diced

2 cups vegetable stock

2 tablespoons vegan Worcestershire sauce

2 tablespoons chopped fresh parsley

2 bay leaves

One 14-ounce can petite diced tomatoes, with juices

2 green onions, chopped, optional

2 cups cooked brown or white rice

Warm the oil in a large saucepan or Dutch oven over medium-high heat. Add the seitan and sausage and cook, stirring often, until they begin to brown, about 10 minutes. Remove from the pan.

Add 3 tablespoons of the margarine to the pan and allow to melt. Add the flour and cook over medium-low heat, stirring constantly, until brown, about 20 minutes.

Add the remaining tablespoon of margarine, then add the onion, garlic, green pepper, and celery and cook for 5 minutes. Stir in the stock, Worcestershire sauce, parsley, and bay leaves and bring to a low simmer. Stir in the seitan and sausage. Bring to a boil, then reduce the heat, cover, and simmer for 10 minutes. Stir in the tomatoes, cover, and simmer for an additional 10 minutes. Just before serving, stir in the green onions, if using. Serve over the rice.

# Naw-Fish Étouffée

**MAKES 6 TO 8 SERVINGS**

Étouffée *is French for "smothered," and this dish lives up to its name. Crawfish étouffée is a New Orleans favorite where the crustacean is smothered in a rich sauce similar to a gumbo but much thicker. There's no way a crawfish is getting anywhere near my kitchen; however, lobster mushrooms give this Naw-Fish Étouffée a fresh-from-the-ocean taste without the cruelty.*

*As in gumbo, roux is the defining characteristic of étouffée. You have two choices of roux for this one: You can go for a dark roux by using margarine, or a reddish roux by using canola oil. If you want an extra-rich dark roux, try cooking in a large cast-iron skillet. For a deep red roux, use a heavy-bottomed skillet.*

¼ cup nonhydrogenated margarine or canola oil

⅓ cup unbleached all-purpose flour

1 cup diced onions

1 celery rib, diced

½ small green bell pepper, diced

½ small red bell pepper, diced

3 garlic cloves, minced

2 cups vegetable stock

½ cup beer

½ teaspoon fine sea salt

¼ teaspoon ground white pepper

1 teaspoon Cajun Spice Blend (page 255)

¼ teaspoon red pepper flakes, or more, depending on desired heat

12 ounces fresh lobster mushrooms (see page 8), sliced thin

¼ cup chopped fresh parsley

3 cups cooked brown or white rice

Melt the margarine in a large cast-iron or heavy-bottomed skillet over medium heat. Stir in the flour and cook, stirring constantly, until a rich brown roux is formed, about 20 minutes.

Stir in the onions, celery, green bell pepper, red bell pepper, and garlic. Cook until tender, 2 to 3 minutes.

Stir in the stock, beer, salt, white pepper, Cajun Spice Blend, red pepper flakes, and lobster mushrooms. Simmer for 15 minutes, then stir in the parsley and simmer for an additional 5 minutes.

Serve the étouffée over the rice.

# Lobster and Cheese Grits

*I'm a California girl through and through. There we eat grits with margarine and sugar or maybe a little salt and pepper for breakfast—they just don't exist outside the breakfast table. Within two weeks of moving to the South, on the other hand, I was served grits for breakfast, lunch, and dinner with everything you could imagine. Here in the South they top grits with cheese, stir in butter and milk, and then top it all off with shrimp, crawfish, salmon, or if you're being really fancy, a little bit of lobster. Bring a little bit of the South to your kitchen with Lobster and Cheese Grits.*

### LOBSTER

¾ cup dry white wine

¼ cup extra-virgin olive oil

¼ cup nonhydrogenated margarine

3 garlic cloves, minced

¼ teaspoon paprika

⅛ teaspoon ground white pepper

1 teaspoon fresh lemon juice

1 pound fresh lobster mushrooms (see page 8)

2 tablespoons chopped fresh parsley

Fine sea salt to taste

### CHEESE GRITS

3 cups water

¾ cup quick-cooking grits

2 tablespoons nonhydrogenated margarine

¼ teaspoon fine sea salt

¼ cup shredded vegan cheddar or mozzarella, or a combination

**TO MAKE THE LOBSTER:** Warm the wine, oil, margarine, and garlic in a large skillet over medium heat until the mixture starts to boil, about 4 to 5 minutes. Stir in the paprika, white pepper, lemon juice, and lobster mushrooms. Cook for an additional 4 to 5 minutes or until the mushrooms start to soften.

Stir in the parsley and season with salt. Remove from the heat and serve alongside the cheese grits, or top the grits with the sautéed lobster mushrooms.

**TO MAKE THE CHEESE GRITS**: Bring the water to a boil in a medium saucepan, then slowly stir in the grits, margarine, and salt. Cover and reduce the heat to medium-low. Cook for 5 minutes or until thickened. Add the cheese and continue to cook until it melts, about 1 minute, stirring occasionally.

# Fried Oysters with Cajun-Spiced Horseradish

**MAKES 4 TO 6 SERVINGS**

*I've never actually had a real oyster, and am a happier person for it, but I've had pounds and pounds of oyster mushrooms in my life. These little gray fungi are my culinary best friends. We take long walks in the park and watch reruns of* The Golden Girls *together, and when the day is done, we sit down to dinner together, where I bread 'em, fry 'em, and dip 'em in a Cajun Horseradish sauce. Without further ado, let me introduce you to my best friend, the Fried Oyster.*

Canola oil for frying

1 cup white rice flour

½ cup cornmeal

1 teaspoon paprika

½ teaspoon cayenne pepper

1 teaspoon fine sea salt

1 cup plain rice or soy milk

1 pound fresh oyster mushrooms (see page 8)

1 recipe Cajun Spiced Horseradish (recipe follows)

Preheat a deep fryer to 375°F or heat about ½ inch of oil in a large frying pan over medium heat. To test the heat, sprinkle a small drop of water into the oil. When the water begins to pop, the oil is ready.

Mix the rice flour, cornmeal, paprika, cayenne, and salt in a small shallow bowl. Pour the milk into a separate shallow bowl.

Dip the mushrooms in the milk, then in the flour mixture, and fry in small batches until golden brown, 2 to 3 minutes. Drain on paper towels. Serve with the Cajun-Spiced Horseradish.

86

# Cajun-Spiced Horseradish

**MAKES ⅔ CUP**

1 teaspoon Cajun Spice Blend (page 255)

¼ cup vegan mayonnaise

¼ cup vegan sour cream

1½ tablespoons unsweetened soy milk

2 tablespoons freshly grated horseradish

Stir all the ingredients together and store in an airtight container in the refrigerator until ready to use. This keeps in the refrigerator for about 4 days.

## Cook's Tip

The longer the Cajun-Spiced Horseradish sits, the better it gets, so feel free to make it a day or so ahead of time for an intense flavor.

# Oyster Po' Boys

Po' boys are sub sandwiches New Orleans–style: crusty French bread stuffed with fried shrimp or oysters. You can eat your po' boy plain with just Fried Oysters and bread, or dressed with mayonnaise, pickles, lettuce, and tomatoes. I prefer mine dressed with a little Ancho Chile Tartar Sauce to give it a smokey bite. Oyster Po' Boys are a great way to turn leftover Fried Oysters (page 86) into a New Orleans tradition.

1 recipe Ancho Chile Tartar Sauce

6 hoagie or French rolls, lightly toasted

1 recipe Fried Oysters (page 86)

Romaine or green leaf lettuce, sliced thin

1 tomato, sliced thin

### ANCHO CHILE TARTAR SAUCE

1½ teaspoon ground ancho chile

¼ teaspoon cayenne pepper

½ cup vegan mayonnaise

¼ cup drained sweet pickle relish

¼ teaspoon yellow mustard

**TO MAKE THE ANCHO CHILE TARTAR SAUCE:** Stir all the ingredients together until thoroughly mixed. Refrigerate for 10 minutes.

**TO MAKE THE SANDWICHES:** Spread the Ancho Chile Tartar Sauce on the hoagie rolls, dividing it evenly. Fill each roll with one-sixth of the fried oysters, lettuce, and tomato.

## Cook's Tip

If using leftover Fried Oysters, feel free to use any leftover Cajun-Spiced Horseradish (page 87) instead of the Ancho Chile Tartar Sauce to dress these po' boys.

# Bourbon Street Tofu

*Bourbon might be a Kentucky tradition, but Bourbon Street is where all the fun happens in New Orleans. Whenever my girl-friends and I hit the city, the first and last place we always go is Bourbon Street. The music is loud, the people are dancing, and everyone is smiling with a Hurricane (page 97) in hand.*

3 tablespoons canola oil

½ small onion, sliced thin

½ red bell pepper, sliced thin

1 garlic clove, minced

½ teaspoon red pepper flakes

1⅓ cups ketchup

2 teaspoons apple cider vinegar

2 teaspoons vegan Worcestershire sauce

1 tablespoon agave nectar

2 teaspoons Bragg Liquid Aminos

⅓ cup loosely packed light brown sugar

¼ teaspoon dry mustard

3 tablespoons bourbon

1 pound extra-firm tofu, pressed and cut into ½-inch cubes

Warm the canola oil in a medium saucepan over medium heat. Add the onion and bell pepper and sauté for 5 minutes or until soft. Add the garlic and sauté for an additional minute. Stir in all the remaining ingredients. Reduce the heat to medium-low, cover, and simmer for 15 minutes, stirring occasionally, until warmed through.

# Dirty Rice

MAKES 4 TO 6 SERVINGS

*The name might not sound too appealing, but the taste says it all. Traditional dirty rice has chicken livers and sausage in it, which are the opposite of appetizing, but this veganized bayou classic uses spicy and smokey Andouille Sausage and a little brown rice, instead of white rice, to make sure it sticks to your ribs. I usually double the batch, as it ends up being my main course every time I make it.*

1 link Andouille Sausage, cut in half (page 76)

2 tablespoons canola oil

2 green onions, chopped

½ cup diced bell pepper

1 celery rib, diced

2 cups cooked brown rice

Fine sea salt to taste

Pulse the sausage in a food processor until you have small crumbles.

Warm the canola oil in a large skillet over medium heat. Add the sausage, green onions, bell pepper, and celery. Cook for 5 minutes. Stir in the rice until well mixed. Remove from the heat, season with salt, and serve.

# Beignets

Beignet *is French for "fried dough." No matter what language you speak, fried dough is never a bad thing. Beignets can be filled with all sorts of sweet and savory treats, from jams and preserves to warm sautéed lobster mushrooms or even a little spoonful of Naw-Fish Étouffée (page 82). But in the city where they have been made famous, New Orleans, they are simply dusted with confectioners' sugar and served warm. Feel free to try all the variations, but remember—if you choose to go with a savory filling, forgo the confectioners' sugar.*

MAKES 18 BEIGNETS

2 cups unsweetened rice, oat, or soy milk

4½ teaspoons active dry yeast

¼ cup granulated sugar

3½ cups unbleached all-purpose flour

2 teaspoons vital wheat gluten

½ teaspoon baking soda

¼ teaspoon fine sea salt

Canola oil for frying

Confectioners' sugar for dusting

Warm the milk in a small saucepan over medium heat for 2 to 3 minutes or until just warmed through. Pour it into the bowl of a stand mixer. Whisk in the yeast and allow to sit for 10 minutes. Add the granulated sugar, flour, vital wheat gluten, baking soda, and salt and mix on low speed, using the dough hook. Scrape down the sides as needed and mix until the ingredients are incorporated. Increase the speed of the mixer to medium and mix until a dough begins to form, 2 to 3 minutes. Scrape the dough off the dough hook, cover the bowl, and allow the dough to rise until double in size. This should take about 1 hour.

Preheat a deep fryer to 375°F or heat about ½ inch of oil in a large frying pan over medium heat. To test the heat, sprinkle a small drop of water into the oil. When the water begins to pop, the oil is ready.

Turn the dough out onto a lightly floured surface and knead for 1 minute. Roll out to ⅛-inch thickness and cut into 1½- to 2-inch squares.

Fry the beignets in small batches until puffed and golden brown, turning halfway through frying, 1 to 2 minutes. Drain on paper towels and continue until the entire batch has been fried. Dust with confectioners' sugar and serve warm.

## Cook's Tip

Use a pizza slicer to cut the beignet squares from the dough.

# Baked Beignets with Chocolate Almond Sauce

*The word* beignet *might mean "fried dough" in French, but to my waistline it translates into little baby love handles. Once in a while I try to make myself feel better by baking my favorite pastries instead of frying them. It lowers the calorie count and makes you feel like you're not eating junk food anymore. However, I must warn you, one taste of this Chocolate Almond Sauce and it will be hard to convince your taste buds that these beignets are anything but pure sin.*

**MAKES 30 BEIGNETS**

¼ cup warm water

2¼ teaspoons active dry yeast

3 cups unbleached all-purpose flour

1½ teaspoons baking powder

½ teaspoon baking soda

½ teaspoon fine sea salt

¼ cup granulated sugar

¼ cup nonhydrogenated margarine

¾ cup plain rice milk

1 egg equivalent prepared Ener-G Egg Replacer (see page 5)

1 recipe Chocolate Almond Sauce (recipe follows)

¼ cup confectioners' sugar

Whisk the warm water with the yeast in small bowl. Stir and let stand until foamy, about 5 minutes.

Stir together the flour, baking powder, baking soda, salt, and granulated sugar in a large bowl. Incorporate the margarine into the flour mixture using a pastry blender or fork to cut it in until the mixture is pebbly.

Whisk the milk and prepared egg replacer into the yeast mixture until blended. Make a well in the flour mixture and pour in the yeast mixture. Stir until combined and a soft dough forms. If the dough appears dry, knead it with your hands in the bowl. When the dough is formed, cover the bowl and let stand for 50 minutes or until the dough doubles in size.

Preheat the oven to 375°F. Line a large baking sheet with parchment paper.

Turn the dough out onto a lightly floured surface. Roll out to ⅛-inch thickness and cut into 1½- to 2-inch squares. Place the squares on the baking sheet about 1 inch apart. Cover and let sit for 20 minutes.

Bake the beignets for 8 to 10 minutes or until golden. While the beignets are baking, make the Chocolate Almond Sauce. Once the beignets are done baking, sprinkle with the confectioners' sugar and serve with the Chocolate Almond Sauce.

## ★Chocolate Almond Sauce

2 tablespoons nonhydrogenated margarine

½ cup sugar

2 tablespoons unsweetened cocoa powder

3 tablespoons water

½ teaspoon almond extract

Melt the margarine in a small saucepan. Whisk in the sugar, cocoa powder, and water and bring to a low boil over medium heat. Boil for 1 minute. Remove from the heat, whisk in the almond extract, and pour into a small bowl.

# King Cake

In Europe king cakes are traditionally eaten around Christmas, but in the States we eat them around Mardi Gras. Because of the king cake's Christmas origins, traditionally a little plastic baby Jesus is hidden inside the cake. However, a plastic baby Jesus tends to be a bit of a choking hazard and therefore is rarely put in king cakes anymore. As tradition goes, whoever finds the baby in the cake has to buy the king cake the next year. Once you make your own king cake, you'll never want a store-bought one again.

## CAKE

2¼ teaspoons active dry yeast

½ cup warm water

4 tablespoons sugar

2 tablespoons nonhydrogenated margarine

1 cup vegan sour cream

½ teaspoon fine sea salt

1 egg equivalent prepared Ener-G Egg Replacer (see page 5)

3¼ cups unbleached all-purpose flour

## FILLING

One 8-ounce package vegan cream cheese

½ cup plus 1 tablespoon confectioners' sugar

Pinch of fine sea salt

## FROSTING

1½ cups confectioners' sugar

1½ tablespoons nonhydrogenated margarine, melted

1½ tablespoons plain rice, oat, or soy milk

¼ teaspoon vanilla extract

2 drops each red, blue, yellow, and green food coloring

**TO MAKE THE CAKE:** Whisk the yeast, warm water, and 1 tablespoon of the sugar together in a small bowl and let stand until foamy, about 5 minutes.

**MAKES 14 SERVINGS**

> ## Cook's Tip
>
> This cake is a breeze to make with a stand mixer, but don't worry if you don't have one—it can easily be made with an electric mixer and a little elbow grease to knead the dough.

While the yeast is proofing, mix the batter. You can use an electric mixer or a stand mixer.

If using an electric mixer, cream the remaining 3 tablespoons sugar with the margarine, sour cream, salt, and prepared egg replacer in a large bowl at high speed. Add the yeast mixture to the sour cream mixture and beat to combine. Slowly incorporate the flour, a heaping ½ cup at a time. Turn the dough out onto a lightly floured surface and knead until smooth and elastic, about 3 minutes. Place the dough in a lightly oiled bowl, cover, and allow to double in size, about 1 hour.

If using a stand mixer, cream the remaining 3 tablespoons sugar, margarine, sour cream, salt, and egg replacer using the dough hook. Add the yeast mixture and the flour, ½ cup at a time. Run for 2 minutes, remove the dough hook, then cover the bowl and let the dough double in size, about 1 hour.

**TO MAKE THE FILLING**: Cream together all the filling ingredients.

**TO BAKE THE CAKE**: Turn the dough out onto a lightly floured surface, knead twice, and roll into an ⅛-inch-thick rectangle (about 12 x 24 inches). Spread with the filling. Roll the dough like a large jelly roll, then place it, seam side down, on a parchment-lined baking sheet. Bring the ends of the dough together to make an oval ring. Cover and allow to rise for 25 minutes.

Preheat the oven to 375°F. Bake for 15 minutes or until golden. Allow to cool completely before frosting.

**TO MAKE THE FROSTING**: Whisk together the confectioners' sugar, margarine, milk, and vanilla in a medium bowl. Divide the frosting among 3 bowls and add 2 drops each of red and blue to the first bowl, 2 drops of yellow to the second, and 2 drops of green to the third. Decorate the cooled cake with 2- to 3-inch bands of frosting in each color.

# Hurricane

*Take a walk down Bourbon Street in New Orleans, and within five minutes you will be offered a hurricane at least five times. Hurricanes are the unofficial drink of New Orleans, and no trip to that magical city (or true New Orleans–style Mardi Gras celebration) would be complete without a Hurricane or two.*

MAKES 4 SERVINGS

½ cup vodka

¼ cup grenadine

½ cup white rum

½ cup dark rum

1½ cups orange juice

1½ cups pineapple juice

Stir all the ingredients together in a pitcher. Pour the Hurricanes over ice into four 16-ounce glasses, preferably hurricane glasses.

# ★ St. Patrick's Day ★

**S**T. PATRICK'S DAY isn't just a day of four-leaf clovers, dyed green rivers, and drunken frat boys running the streets. It's actually a holiday with deep Christian roots—after all, there is a *saint* in the name. St. Patrick is the patron saint of Ireland, and the holiday developed over the years as a celebration around his feast day. St. Patrick's Day crossed the pond from Ireland to the United States in 1737, with the first public celebration in Boston—and as you can see, the party is still going strong all across the country. This St. Patrick's Day, indulge in the culinary riches of Ireland with comfort foods like Shepherd's Pie and Irish Soda Bread, and put a new twist on some age-old favorites with dishes like Red Potato Cakes with Tomato and Wilted Spinach or Stout Beer Cupcakes with Whiskey Cream Cheeze Frosting.

Irish Soda Bread

Red Potato Cakes with Tomato And Wilted Spinach

Shepherd's Pie

Fish and Chips

Tempeh Reuben Sandwiches

Red Cabbage Salad

Stout Beer Cupcakes with Whiskey Cream Cheeze Frosting

Green Velvet Cupcakes

Irish Cream Liqueur

Irish Cream Latte

St. Patty's Shake

# Irish Soda Bread

**MAKES ONE 9-INCH LOAF**

*If you scan the list of ingredients for Irish Soda Bread, you'll notice that there isn't any soda in it except baking soda. This bread actually gets its name from that little ½ teaspoon of baking soda, which, along with baking powder, helps it rise and eliminates the need for yeast. Traditional Irish soda bread doesn't use dried fruit or caraway seeds, but in the States the addition of these two ingredients has become a deliciously important part of the recipe that I couldn't imagine leaving out.*

3½ cups unbleached all-purpose flour

½ cup sugar

½ teaspoon baking soda

4 teaspoons baking powder

1 teaspoon fine sea salt

1½ cups vegan sour cream

1 cup plain rice or soy milk

2 tablespoons white vinegar

1 tablespoon caraway seeds

½ cup raisins, dried sweetened cranberries, or dried currants

Preheat the oven to 350°F. Grease a 9-inch springform pan with shortening or oil.

Mix the flour, sugar, baking soda, baking powder, and salt in a large bowl.

Whisk the sour cream, milk, and vinegar in a small bowl.

Add the sour cream mixture, caraway seeds, and raisins to the dry ingredients, stirring until a dough forms. Feel free to dig in with your hands and knead the dough together if need be.

Transfer the dough to the prepared pan.

Bake for 50 minutes or until golden brown and a knife comes out clean.

# Red Potato Cakes
## with Tomato and Wilted Spinach

*Every time I make this dish, I struggle to decide whether to serve it for breakfast, lunch, or dinner. But it's so darn good I usually end up eating it at every meal. For breakfast it pairs great with a Broccoli Frittata (page 116), for lunch with Fish and Chips, minus the chips (page 104), and for dinner I love it with Panfried Seitan with White Wine Herb Sauce (page 62).*

**MAKES 6 CAKES**

1 pound new red potatoes, scrubbed and chopped

1 small zucchini, diced

1 small yellow squash, diced

3 tablespoons plain soy or rice milk

½ teaspoon fine sea salt

6 tablespoons extra-virgin olive oil

6 cups fresh baby spinach

1 large tomato, sliced ¼ inch thick

Put the potatoes in a large saucepan and cover with water. Bring to a boil and cook for 10 minutes or until tender. Drain and transfer to a large bowl. Lightly mash the potatoes, leaving some large chunks.

Add the zucchini, squash, milk, and salt to the potatoes and stir to combine. Form the potato mixture into 6 balls, using about ½ cup of the mixture for each, then lightly flatten to form cakes.

Heat 4 tablespoons of the oil in a large griddle or skillet over medium heat. Add the potato cakes and fry on both sides until lightly browned, 3 to 4 minutes on each side.

Warm the remaining 2 tablespoons of oil in a separate large saucepan. Add the spinach and sauté until it has wilted down. Remove from the heat.

You can either serve the tomato slices raw or roast them under the broiler for 2 to 3 minutes.

To assemble, lay out the tomatoes on serving plates. Top with the potato cakes, and then with the wilted spinach.

# Shepherd's Pie

*Shepherd's Pie is the ultimate one-pot meal. It has everything you need—a concentrated protein source and colorful vegetables all topped with a blanket of fluffy mashed potatoes. Master chefs would scoff at the use of instant mashed potatoes in a dish. But for the home cook it is a wonderful, practical option to cut down the prep and cook time of a traditional shepherd's pie and make it a truly quick and easy dish.*

**POTATO TOPPING**

2 cups water

½ teaspoon fine sea salt

2 tablespoons nonhydrogenated margarine

1 cup plain soy milk

2 cups plain instant mashed potato flakes

**FILLING**

1 cup dark vegetable stock

1½ teaspoons hickory liquid smoke

1 cup textured vegetable protein (TVP)

2 tablespoons canola oil

1 cup diced white onions

2 medium carrots, peeled and diced

2 garlic cloves, minced

½ teaspoon fine sea salt

½ teaspoon ground black pepper

2 tablespoons unbleached all-purpose flour

1 tablespoon ketchup

1½ cups light vegetable stock

1 teaspoon vegan Worcestershire sauce

1 teaspoon dried rosemary

1 teaspoon dried thyme

1 teaspoon paprika

2 bay leaves

1 cup fresh or frozen and thawed green beans, cut into 1-inch pieces

**TO MAKE THE POTATO TOPPING**: Bring the water, salt, and margarine to a boil in a medium saucepan over medium-high heat. Remove from the heat and stir in the milk, and then the potatoes. Stir until the ingredients are incorporated and you have a saucepan full of mashed potatoes.

**TO MAKE THE FILLING**: Bring the dark stock and liquid smoke to a boil in a small pot. Remove from the heat, stir in the TVP, and let sit for 5 minutes.

Preheat the oven to 400° F. Line a baking sheet with foil.

Warm the oil in a medium saucepan over medium heat. Add the onions and carrots and sauté until the carrots begin to brighten, 3 to 4 minutes. Add the garlic and stir to combine. Add the rehydrated TVP, salt, and pepper and cook another 3 minutes. Sprinkle the flour over the TVP mixture and toss to coat, continuing to cook for another minute. Add the ketchup, light vegetable stock, Worcestershire sauce, rosemary, thyme, paprika, and bay leaves and stir to combine. Bring to a boil, reduce the heat to low, cover, and simmer slowly for 10 to 12 minutes or until thickened.

Add the green beans to the TVP mixture and stir to combine. Remove the bay leaves and spread the mixture evenly into a 2-quart casserole dish. Top with the mashed potatoes, seal the edges to prevent the filling from bubbling up, and smooth with a spatula. Place the casserole on the foil-lined baking sheet and bake for 25 minutes or just until the potatoes begin to brown. Remove from the oven and allow to cool for 10 minutes before serving.

## Cook's Tip

I like to use an ovenproof 2-quart Dutch oven when making the filling for this dish so I can transfer the pie straight from the stovetop to the oven. If you'd like to use a Dutch oven, skip the step of transferring the mixture into a casserole dish before baking It.

# Fish and Chips

*This recipe has a lot of components to it, but if you get all the ingredients together ahead of time then it all goes smoothly and fairly quickly. If you're in a hurry you can fry the chips instead of baking them, but baking them cuts the amount of fried food in this recipe in half.*

**BROTH**

2½ cups water

½ teaspoon fine sea salt

½ teaspoon kelp granules

1 tablespoon nutritional yeast

⅛ teaspoon cayenne pepper

**SEITAN**

½ cup vital wheat gluten

¼ cup soy flour

¼ teaspoon kelp powder

½ cup water

**FISH**

Canola oil for frying

½ cup whole wheat pastry flour

¼ cup unbleached all-purpose flour

¼ teaspoon garlic powder

¼ teaspoon onion powder

1 teaspoon paprika

½ teaspoon fine sea salt

¼ teaspoon ground black pepper

1 cup plain soy, rice, or hemp milk

1 recipe Chips (recipe follows)

**TO MAKE THE BROTH**: Put the 2 cups of water and the salt, kelp granules, nutritional yeast, and cayenne in a medium saucepan and bring to a boil.

**TO MAKE THE SEITAN:** Stir the vital wheat gluten, soy flour, and kelp powder together in a small bowl until combined, then add the ½ cup of water. Stir until it forms into a ball.

Pinch off 1-inch pieces of dough and place them in the boiling broth, being careful not to splash the hot broth.

Reduce the heat, cover, and simmer until all the broth has been absorbed, 30 to 40 minutes, stirring every 10 minutes.

**TO MAKE THE FISH:** Preheat a deep fryer to 375°F or heat about ½ inch of oil in a large frying pan over medium heat. To test the heat, sprinkle a small drop of water into the oil. When the water begins to pop, the oil is ready.

Mix the whole wheat pastry flour, all-purpose flour, garlic powder, onion powder, paprika, salt, and pepper in a shallow dish.

Pour the milk into a separate shallow dish.

Dredge the seitan in the flour mixture, then the milk, and then back in the flour.

Fry the seitan in small batches until brown on both sides, 2 to 3 minutes on each side. Remove from the oil and drain on paper towels. Serve with Chips (below).

# Chips

>
> 2 large Yukon Gold potatoes,
>   scrubbed and cut into thin strips
>
> ½ teaspoon fine sea salt
>
> ¼ teaspoon paprika
>
> 1 tablespoon canola oil

Preheat the oven to 400°F. Cover a baking sheet with nonstick foil and lightly oil it.

Put all the ingredients in a large bowl and toss to coat the potatoes. Transfer to the prepared baking sheet and bake for 20 to 25 minutes or until crispy.

# Tempeh Reuben Sandwiches

*It is hard to determine the origin of the first Reuben sandwich. Some say it was from Germany, others say Ohio, others New York, and others Ireland or England. Wherever it started, it has become a staple in Irish pubs and a beloved St. Patty's Day sandwich in the States. In my opinion, it's the best thing that ever happened to rye bread, no matter where it came from.*

2 tablespoons canola oil

One 8-ounce package tempeh, any variety, sliced into thin strips

½ small white or sweet yellow onion, sliced thin

1 cup vegetable stock

1 bay leaf

½ teaspoon fennel seed

½ teaspoon dried dill

¼ teaspoon garlic powder

⅛ teaspoon ground white pepper

8 slices rye bread

Nonhydrogenated margarine for the bread

Prepared sauerkraut

1 recipe Thousand Island Dressing (page 250)

Warm the canola oil in a medium skillet over medium heat. Add the tempeh and onion and sauté for 5 minutes or until the tempeh is slightly browned and the onion is translucent. Add the stock, bay leaf, fennel seed, dill, garlic powder, and pepper and cook until the liquid is absorbed, 12 to 15 minutes. Remove the bay leaf.

Spread each slice of bread with margarine. On a large griddle or skillet over medium-high heat, place the bread margarine side down and grill until lightly browned, about 2 minutes. Place 4 slices of bread grilled side down and top with tempeh, sauerkraut, and Thousand Island Dressing, then add the remaining slices of bread, grilled side up. Cut the sandwiches in half and serve.

# Red Cabbage Salad

*This is a simple, sweet, and crunchy salad that pairs well with Tempeh Reuben Sandwiches (page 106).*

**MAKES 4 TO 6 SERVINGS**

½ red cabbage, sliced into thin strips

1 large carrot, shredded

¼ cup agave nectar

½ cup apple cider vinegar

2 tablespoons Bragg Liquid Aminos

Place the cabbage and carrot in a large bowl.

Whisk the agave nectar, vinegar, and liquid aminos in a separate small bowl. Pour over the cabbage mixture and mix well. Cover the bowl or transfer to an airtight container and refrigerate overnight or for at least 8 hours. Serve cold.

# Stout Beer Cupcakes with Whiskey Cream Cheeze Frosting

**MAKES 24 CUPCAKES**

*These cupcakes are not for the kiddos—they are velvety, choco-latey goodness laced with an Irish stout beer and topped with fluffy Irish Whiskey Cream Cheese Frosting. A perfect way to end a phenomenal Irish meal and start your St. Patrick's Day party off right.*

12 ounces stout beer

½ cup canola oil

½ cup plain rice, soy, almond, or oat milk

2 teaspoons vanilla extract

¾ cup vegan sour cream

¼ cup unsweetened applesauce

1 tablespoon apple cider vinegar

¾ cup unsweetened cocoa powder

1 cup loosely packed light brown sugar

1 cup granulated sugar

1 teaspoon baking powder

2½ teaspoons baking soda

2½ cups unbleached all-purpose flour

1 recipe Whiskey Cream Cheeze Frosting (recipe follows)

Preheat the oven to 350°F. Line two 12-cup cupcake tins with paper baking cups.

Whisk the beer, oil, milk, vanilla, sour cream, applesauce, and vinegar in a large bowl until well mixed. Add the cocoa powder, brown sugar, and granulated sugar and whisk until smooth.

Stir in the baking powder, baking soda, and 1 cup of the flour until fully incorporated. Add the remaining 1½ cups of flour and stir until the batter is smooth.

Divide the batter among the cupcake pans, filling each cup about three-quarters full. Bake one pan at a time for 23 to 25 minutes or until a toothpick comes out clean. Allow the cup-cakes to cool completely before frosting with the Whiskey Cream Cheeze Frosting.

# Whiskey Cream Cheeze Frosting

**MAKES 2 CUPS**

One 8-ounce package vegan cream cheese

1½ cups confectioners' sugar

¼ cup shortening

¼ cup nonhydrogenated margarine, softened

2 tablespoons Irish whiskey

Mix all the ingredients together with an electric mixer until smooth and fluffy. Spread evenly over the completely cooled cupcakes.

**Cook's Tip**

I'm not a whiskey drinker, but I can't imagine these cupcakes without the Whiskey Cream Cheeze Frosting. If you're anything like me, you can forgo buying a big bottle of Irish whiskey and opt for the mini bottles. They have just the right amount of whiskey.

# Green Velvet Cupcakes

**MAKES 24 CUPCAKES**

*Stout Beer Cupcakes with Whiskey Cream Cheeze Frosting (page 108) might not exactly be kid friendly, so while the adults are enjoying their liquor-laced cupcakes, try these fun green cupcakes for the kids.*

2½ cups unbleached all-purpose flour

1 teaspoon baking soda

½ teaspoon baking powder

1 teaspoon fine sea salt

1 tablespoon unsweetened cocoa powder

1½ cups sugar

1 cup nonhydrogenated margarine, softened

½ cup shortening

1 cup plain soy, oat, or rice milk

¼ cup unsweetened applesauce

¼ cup plain soy yogurt

½ teaspoon green food coloring

1 teaspoon vanilla extract

1 recipe Cream Cheeze Frosting (page 246)

Preheat the oven to 350°F. Line two 12-cup cupcake tins with paper baking cups.

Sift the flour, baking soda, baking powder, salt, and cocoa powder into a medium bowl.

In a separate large bowl, cream the sugar, margarine, and shortening with an electric mixer on high speed. Add the milk, beating well. Add the applesauce, yogurt, food coloring, and vanilla, beating well.

Add the flour mixture a heaping ½ cup at a time, beating well after each addition.

Divide the batter among the cupcake tins, filling each cup approximately three-quarters full. Bake one pan at a time until a toothpick comes out clean, about 20 minutes.

Allow the cupcakes to cool completely, then frost with Cream Cheeze Frosting.

# Irish Cream Liqueur

*Folks are always surprised to discover that most alcoholic beverages are, indeed, vegan. However, Irish creams aren't one of them. Don't fret—creating your own Irish Cream Liqueur at home is as easy as whisking together five common ingredients. After all, what would St. Patrick's Day be without a traditional Irish cream?*

**MAKES 2 CUPS**

1 cup canned coconut milk

2 tablespoons agave nectar

½ teaspoon vanilla extract

½ cup Irish whiskey

¼ teaspoon unsweetened cocoa powder

Whisk together all the ingredients. If not using immediately, store the liqueur in an airtight container (a Mason jar works perfectly) in the refrigerator.

# Irish Cream Latte

**MAKES ONE 12-OUNCE LATTE**

*In March, one half of the United States is sunny and warm, and the other half, the half I live on, is wet and rainy. On those wet and rainy nights there's nothing better than a warm cup of joe with a little Irish cream and almond milk. I love sipping on this Irish Cream Latte while nibbling on Stout Beer Cupcakes with Whiskey Cream Cheeze Frosting (page 108). It's the perfect way to end a St. Patrick's Day celebration.*

1 shot espresso
6 tablespoons Irish Cream Liqueur (page 111)
1 cup warm plain rice, soy, or almond milk

Stir together the espresso, liqueur, and warm milk. Drink it warm.

# St. Patty's Shake

*I think in my entire pre-vegan life I only had three milkshakes, but as a vegan my relationship with milkshakes has grown exponentially and they are one of my favorite quick and easy treats. For St. Patrick's Day I love this thick, green, minty shake. It's a perfect treat for kids and for adults. If you'd like to add a little kick to it, throw in a couple shots of Irish Cream Liqueur (page 111) to turn this into a more adult beverage.*

**MAKES 4 SERVINGS**

1 recipe Vanilla Bean Ice Cream (page 243)

2 cups plain soy or rice milk

¼ teaspoon mint extract

8 drops green food coloring

Put all the ingredients into a blender and blend until smooth. Transfer to serving glasses and serve immediately.

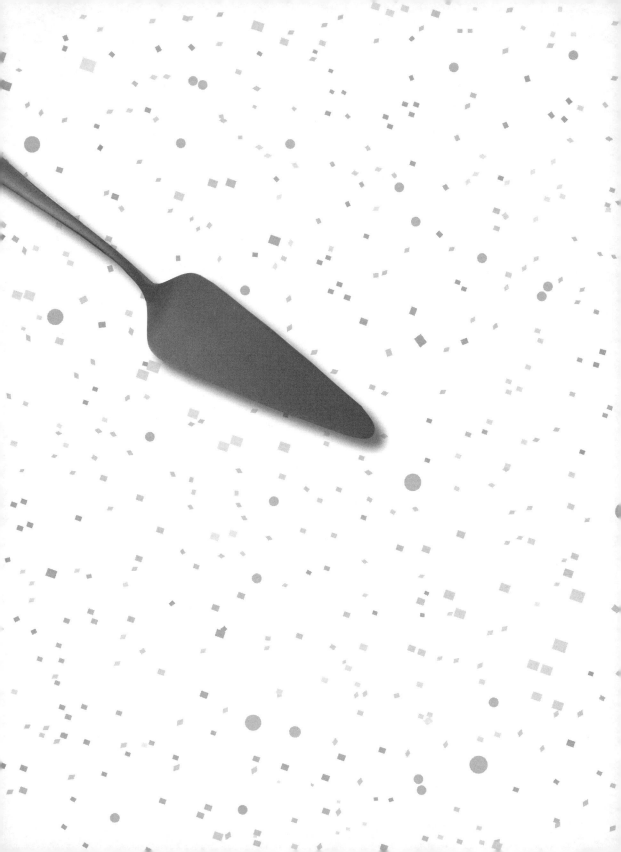

# ★ Easter ★

I LOVE ALL THE traditions that go along with Easter: Easter baskets, Easter egg hunts (with plastic eggs, of course), and my all-time favorite—a new Easter outfit. My nana used to buy me huge, fussy Easter dresses with big ruffled sleeves and skirts, and I love continuing the tradition every year on my own—sans ruffles, of course. But the best tradition of them all is gathering around the table with family, giving thanks, and celebrating.

Easter is also the perfect time to welcome a new companion animal into your life. If you have room in your heart and your home for a bunny, animal shelters are usually flooded with bunnies right after Easter. Unfortunately, many people don't realize how big a responsibility bunnies are as companion animals and end up surrendering them after buying Easter bunnies for their children. But hard work aside, they are wonderful companion animals. Cunningham, my shelter bunny, is without a doubt one of the cutest and sweetest additions to my fur family.

Broccoli Frittata

Rosemary and Chive Biscuits

Hidden Treasure Muffins

Crispy Baked Tofu

Creamy Broccoli and Cauliflower Soup

Parmesan Roasted Asparagus

Au Gratin Potatoes

Creamed Corn

Hummingbird Cupcakes

# Broccoli Frittata

*Thanksgiving isn't the only holiday where you spend the entire day eating. In my home, Easter brunch is mandatory, and in my opinion, nothing says brunch like a veggie-filled frittata. Pair this with Rosemary and Chive Biscuits (page 118) or Hidden Treasure Muffins (page 119) and a little fresh fruit, and you have a delicious, filling brunch.*

Two 12.3-ounce packages extra-firm silken tofu

1 tablespoon tahini

3 tablespoons potato starch or cornstarch

1 teaspoon fine sea salt

¼ teaspoon turmeric

½ teaspoon onion powder

½ cup nutritional yeast

¼ teaspoon dry mustard

¼ teaspoon original Spike Seasoning

2 tablespoons canola oil, plus more for greasing the pan

½ cup diced white onion

½ large red bell pepper, diced

2 garlic cloves, minced

2 cups broccoli florets, steamed and roughly chopped

Put the tofu, tahini, potato starch, salt, turmeric, onion powder, nutritional yeast, mustard, and Spike in a blender and blend until smooth. Pour into a large bowl.

Preheat the oven to 375° F. Grease a 9-inch springform pan with canola oil or shortening.

Warm the oil over medium to medium-high heat in a large skillet. Add the onion and bell pepper and sauté for 3 to 4 minutes or until the onion is translucent. Add the garlic and sauté for an additional 2 to 3 minutes. Add the broccoli and stir to combine.

Stir the vegetables into the tofu mixture.

Pour the tofu mixture into the prepared pan and bake for 35 to 40 minutes or until firm and a toothpick comes out clean.

Cool for 10 to 15 minutes. Remove the frittata from the pan and serve. This can be served warm, at room temperature, or cold.

# Rosemary and Chive Biscuits

**MAKES 10 BISCUITS**

*Rosemary and Chive Biscuits scream brunch. These biscuits aren't made for jam or jelly—just a little Earth Balance margarine and a slice of Broccoli Frittata (page 115) is all you need to make your Easter brunch complete.*

2 cups unbleached all-purpose flour

1 tablespoon baking powder

1 teaspoon fine sea salt

2 tablespoons shortening

2 tablespoons nonhydrogenated margarine

1 cup plus 1 tablespoon plain oat, rice, or soy milk

1 cup vegan mozzarella

2 tablespoons chopped fresh rosemary

2 tablespoons chopped chives

Preheat the oven to 400°F. Grease a baking sheet with shortening or oil.

Put the flour, baking powder, salt, shortening, and margarine into a food processor and pulse until the mixture resembles coarse cornmeal.

Transfer the mixture to a medium bowl, make a well in the center, and add the milk, mozzarella, rosemary, and chives. Stir to combine.

Put the dough on a lightly floured surface and roll out to about ½ inch thick. Cut out biscuits with a biscuit cutter or the mouth of an 8-ounce drinking glass and place on the prepared baking sheet. Collect any scraps, roll out again, and continue to cut biscuits until dough is completely used. Bake for 10 to 12 minutes or until a toothpick comes out clean.

# Hidden Treasure Mu

*Hidden inside these sweet, fluffy treats are all the fruits, vegetables, and whole grains you can pack into one little muffin.*

**MAKES 12 MUFFINS**

1 cup whole wheat pastry flour

½ cup unbleached all-purpose flour

1 cup quick-cooking oats

2 teaspoons baking powder

½ teaspoon baking soda

¼ teaspoon ground nutmeg

½ teaspoon ground cinnamon

1 cup unsweetened applesauce

½ cup plain rice milk

½ cup sweet potato purée

½ cup loosely packed light brown sugar

¼ cup nonhydrogenated margarine, softened

1 tablespoon apple cider vinegar

**STREUSEL**

⅔ cup quick-cooking oats

¼ cup loosely packed light brown sugar

½ teaspoon ground cinnamon

¼ teaspoon ground nutmeg

2 tablespoons canola oil

Preheat the oven to 400°F. Line a 12-cup muffin tin with paper baking cups.

**TO MAKE THE MUFFINS**: Mix the flours, oats, baking powder, baking soda, nutmeg, and cinnamon in a large bowl.

Whisk together the remaining muffin ingredients in a separate small bowl. Add to the flour mixture and stir to combine. Divide the batter evenly among the muffin cups.

**TO MAKE THE STREUSEL**: Mix all the streusel ingredients in a small bowl, then sprinkle evenly over the muffins.

Bake for 22 to 25 minutes or until a toothpick comes out clean.

# Crispy Baked Tofu

MAKES 4 SERVINGS

*I love super-firm tofu. It is firmer than extra-firm tofu, it doesn't need to be pressed or drained, and its texture is amazing. I can't always find super-firm tofu in Atlanta, but when I go home to California it's always available and I make multiple batches of this dish whenever possible. This recipe was the first tofu recipe to win my family over. The texture of the super-firm tofu plus the crispiness of the crust will please even the most die-hard tofu hater.*

Canola oil cooking spray

½ cup plain soy or rice milk

⅛ teaspoon hot sauce or sriracha

1 tablespoon arrowroot

¾ cup panko bread crumbs

2 tablespoons unbleached all-purpose flour

1 teaspoon poultry seasoning

¾ teaspoon paprika

1 teaspoon fine sea salt

¼ cup nutritional yeast

1½ teaspoons onion powder

½ teaspoon garlic powder

¼ teaspoon sugar

¼ teaspoon dried thyme

⅛ teaspoon turmeric

10 ounces super-firm tofu, cut into ½-inch-thick slices

Preheat the oven to 400°F. Cover a baking sheet with foil and spray with canola oil.

Whisk together the milk, hot sauce, and arrowroot.

Put the panko, flour, poultry seasoning, paprika, salt, nutritional yeast, onion powder, garlic powder, sugar, thyme, and turmeric in a shallow dish and mix well.

Dip each slice of tofu in the milk mixture, then in the bread crumb mixture, then back in the milk mixture, and then back in the bread crumb mixture. Place each slice of tofu on the prepared baking sheet. Spray the tops with canola oil and bake until crispy, about 40 minutes.

## Cook's Tip

If super-firm tofu isn't available in your area, use extra-firm tofu that has been pressed overnight using the TofuXpress (page 29) to get the best super-firm tofu texture.

# Creamy Broccoli and Cauliflower Soup

**MAKES 4 SERVINGS**

*There's something about a soup course that makes me feel like I'm eating a big fancy dinner. Unlike most soups, this one won't ruin your meal by leaving you feeling stuffed at the end. It's creamy without being heavy and packs a ton of veggies into one bowl of soup.*

2 tablespoons canola oil

½ cup diced white onion

3 celery ribs, diced

1 garlic clove, minced

3 cups broccoli florets

½ head medium cauliflower, cut in florets

1¼ cups water

1¼ cups vegetable stock

1 teaspoon fine sea salt

Freshly ground black pepper to taste

Warm the canola oil in a large saucepan over medium heat. Add the onion and celery and sauté until the vegetables have softened, about 5 minutes. Add the garlic and sauté for an additional minute, making sure the garlic doesn't burn. Stir in the broccoli, cauliflower, water, and stock and bring to a boil. Reduce the heat, cover, and simmer for 10 minutes or until the cauliflower is tender.

Transfer the soup to a blender and purée until smooth. Stir in the salt and season with pepper. Serve warm.

# Parmesan Roasted Asparagus

*Vegan Parmesan adds a rich flavor to roasted asparagus. My favorite vegan Parmesan cheese for this recipe is Parma brand. I love its simple combination of walnuts, nutritional yeast, and sea salt, making a deliciously rich soy-free Parmesan that adds the perfect touch of flavor to this recipe.*

**MAKES 4 SERVINGS**

1 pound asparagus, ends trimmed

1 tablespoon extra-virgin olive oil

¼ teaspoon fine sea salt

1 tablespoon vegan Parmesan

Preheat the oven to 425°F. Line a baking sheet with foil.

Arrange the asparagus in a single layer on the baking sheet and drizzle the olive oil over it to coat. Sprinkle with the salt and roast for 12 to 15 minutes or until tender.

Remove from the oven and sprinkle with the Parmesan.

# Au Gratin Potatoes

**MAKES 4 TO 6 SERVINGS**

*It's important for this recipe that the potato slices are cut uniformly, and there's no better way to ensure this than to use a mandoline. You don't have to buy one of those $100 French mandolines from a fancy-schmancy specialty store. Your typical home goods store will have them in their kitchen section, usually for under $10.*

3 large Yukon Gold potatoes (about 1½ pounds), peeled and sliced thin

½ yellow or white onion, sliced thin

⅔ cup nutritional yeast

¼ cup canola oil

2 cups unsweetened rice milk

2 tablespoons cornstarch

½ teaspoon paprika

1 teaspoon garlic powder

1 teaspoon fine sea salt

¼ teaspoon ground black pepper

1 teaspoon dried parsley

Preheat the oven to 375°F. Lightly oil a 2-quart casserole dish.

Layer the potatoes and onion in the dish and set aside.

Whisk together the remaining ingredients and pour over the potatoes. Cover with foil and bake for 35 minutes. Uncover and bake for an additional 5 minutes. The potatoes will be very hot, so cool them for about 5 minutes at room temperature before serving.

*Black-Eyed Peas* (page 39), *Cabbage* (page 40), **and** *Southern Sweet Corn Bread* (page 41)

*Tempeh Cakes with Spicy Remoulade* (page 34)

*Loaded Potato Skins* (page 48)

*Game Day Nachos* (page 52)

*Seitan Parmesan* (page 58) and *Garlic Green Beans* (page 68)

*Gingered Champagne Cocktail* (page 42)
and *Sweetheart Sangria* (page 73)

*Red Velvet Cupcakes* (page 70)

*Red Potato Cakes with Tomato and Wilted Spinach* (page 101)

*Fish and Chips* (page 104)

*Crispy Baked Tofu* (page 120), *Parmesan Roasted Asparagus* (page 123), **and** *Roasted Garlic Smashed Potatoes* (page 180)

*Au Gratin Potatoes* (page 124)

*Quinoa Stuffed Poblanos with Black Beans and Mango Peach Salsa* (page 138)

*Tempeh Soft Tacos with Lime Crema* (page 137) **and** *Classic Margarita* (page 145)

*Barbecue Tempeh Hoagies with Chipotle Mayo* (page 148)

*Patriotic Parfait* (page 154)

*Mummy Mini Pizzas* (page 162)

*Severed Fingers* (page 160) and
*Orange O'Lanterns* (page 163)

*Raw Sweet Potato Pie* (page 185)          *Classic Macaroni and Cheeze* (page 174)

*Portobello Brisket* (page 188) and *Roasted Vegetables* (page 189)

*Agave-Glazed Acorn Squash* (page 205)

*Christmas Tamales* (page 202)

*African Peanut Soup* (page 228)          *North African Meatballs* (page 220)

*French Toast with Maple Ice Cream* (page 232)

*Spinach Artichoke Dip* (Game Day, page 50), *Roasted Five-Spice Nuts* (Game Day, page 54), *Spaghetti and Mock Meatballs* (Valentine's Day, page 64), *Creamy Broccoli and Cauliflower Soup* (Easter, page 122), **and** *Chocolate Macadamia Nut Cookies* (Christmas, page 214)

# Creamed Corn

This recipe is strictly about the corn. The use of fresh corn allows you to use all parts of the corn, even the cob, to create a great creamy texture. If you can find both white and yellow corn, then I highly recommend using six ears of each to add another layer of flavor. This dish is sure to be a hit this Easter holiday.

**MAKES 6 TO 8 SERVINGS**

12 ears corn

2 cups water

2 tablespoons nonhydrogenated margarine

1 teaspoon sugar

1 teaspoon fine sea salt

¼ teaspoon ground black pepper

1 cup vegan cream

2 teaspoons unbleached all-purpose flour

Cut the kernels from the cobs, reserving three cobs. Put the corn and reserved cobs in a large saucepan and add the water, margarine, sugar, salt, and pepper. Simmer uncovered over medium heat, stirring occasionally, until the corn is tender, 5 to 7 minutes. Remove the cobs.

Whisk in the cream and flour. Boil over medium heat, whisking constantly, for 1 minute.

Transfer 2 cups of the corn mixture to a blender and purée. Stir the purée back into the corn and simmer for 5 minutes. Serve warm.

# Hummingbird Cupcakes

MAKES 24 CUPCAKES

*My first encounter with hummingbird cake was at a twenty-four-hour diner in Atlanta called R. Thomas Deluxe Grill. I saw it on the menu and was intrigued; however, as the server described the list of ingredients to me, I became perplexed. How could so many different fruits and nuts go into one cake and still be good? Always up for an adventure, I tried a slice and fell in love. Just as I fell in love that night, your guests are sure to fall in love at first bite when they try their first hummingbird cupcake.*

3 cups unbleached all-purpose flour

1 teaspoon baking soda

2 teaspoons baking powder

½ teaspoon ground cinnamon

¼ teaspoon ground nutmeg

½ teaspoon fine sea salt

1 cup nonhydrogenated margarine, softened

2 teaspoons vanilla extract

2 cups sugar

1 tablespoon apple cider vinegar

1 tablespoon plain rice, soy, oat, or almond milk

¼ cup pumpkin purée

¼ cup unsweetened applesauce

1 cup mashed ripe bananas (approximately 3 bananas)

1 cup crushed pineapple

1 cup chopped pecans

1 cup unsweetened shredded coconut

1 recipe Cream Cheeze Frosting (page 246)

Preheat the oven to 350°F. Line two 12-cup cupcake tins with paper baking cups.

Stir together the flour, baking soda, baking powder, cinnamon, nutmeg, and salt in a medium bowl.

Cream the margarine, vanilla, sugar, vinegar, and milk with an electric mixer in a separate bowl. Beat until smooth. Add the pumpkin and applesauce and beat until smooth. Stir in the bananas, pineapple, pecans, and coconut. Add the flour mixture 1 cup at a time, beating well after each addition.

Divide the batter evenly among the cupcake tins, filling each cup about three-quarters full. Bake one pan at a time for 25 to 30 minutes or until golden brown and a toothpick comes out clean.

Cool completely before frosting with the Cream Cheeze Frosting.

# ★ Cinco de Mayo ★

**P**EOPLE IN THE United States tend to equate Cinco de Mayo with Mexico's Independence Day. However, Mexico's Independence Day is actually September 16. Cinco de Mayo is the date of the 1862 Mexican victory over the French in the Battle of Puebla. Over the years, Cinco de Mayo has become a day of celebration in the United States even though it's not considered to be a very big holiday in Mexico.

Admittedly, I'm partial to Cinco de Mayo. It is, hands down, my favorite holiday of the year. I have an annual Cinco de Mayo party at my house filled with my favorite Mexican foods and, of course, pitchers and pitchers of margaritas. I awake the morning of Cinco de Mayo like a kid on Christmas day, ready to unwrap the culinary treats of Mexico from morning to night. Over the years other Latin-influenced dishes have crept into my repertoire for the occasion, but the sentiment I have for this day will never change. I simply love Cinco de Mayo.

Huevos Rancheros

Papa Chorizo Frittata

Flautas sin Pollo

Taco Soup

Tempeh Soft Tacos with Lime Crema

Quinoa-Stuffed Poblanos with Black Beans and Mango Peach Salsa

Chipotle Black Bean Burgers

Chorizo Empanadas

Mexican Chocolate Mousse

Classic Margarita

Frozen Mango Margarita

Pineapple Margarita

# Huevos Rancheros

MAKES 4 SERVINGS

*I celebrate Cinco de Mayo from sunup to sundown, and there's no better way to start your day off than with Mexico's traditional huevos rancheros—an incredible combination of tortillas, salsa, black beans, and, of course, a delicious vegan "egg."*

**HUEVOS**

> 2 tablespoons canola oil
>
> 1 cup diced green bell pepper
>
> 2 garlic cloves, minced
>
> ½ cup diced onion
>
> Two 12.3-ounce packages firm silken tofu
>
> ¼ teaspoon turmeric
>
> 1 teaspoon fine sea salt
>
> 1⅓ cups plain rice or soy milk
>
> 2 to 4 chipotle peppers in adobo sauce, minced

**RANCHERO SAUCE**

> One 14.5-ounce can diced tomatoes
>
> 1 tablespoon canola oil
>
> ½ cup diced white onion
>
> 1 garlic clove, minced
>
> 2 teaspoons dried oregano
>
> 1 teaspoon fine sea salt
>
> ½ teaspoon red pepper flakes
>
> Twelve 6-inch corn tortillas
>
> 2 cups cooked black beans

Preheat the oven to 350°F. Grease a 12-cup cupcake tin.

**TO MAKE THE HUEVOS:** Warm the oil in a medium saucepan over medium heat. Add the bell pepper, garlic, and onion and cook for 5 minutes, stirring occasionally.

Purée the tofu, turmeric, salt, and milk in a blender or food processor until smooth. Transfer the tofu mixture to a medium bowl and stir in the bell pepper mixture and the chipotles.

Divide the egg mixture evenly among the cupcake cups and bake for 35 to 40 minutes or until a toothpick comes out clean. Cool slightly, then remove the "egg" from each cup with a soup spoon.

**TO MAKE THE RANCHERO SAUCE:** Purée the tomatoes in a blender or food processor.

Warm the oil in a medium saucepan over medium heat. Add the onion and garlic and sauté for 2 to 3 minutes.

Stir in the tomatoes, oregano, salt, and red pepper flakes, reduce the heat, cover, and simmer for 15 to 20 minutes while your "egg" is baking.

**TO ASSEMBLE THE HUEVOS RANCHEROS:** Arrange the corn tortillas on serving plates and evenly distribute the cooked black beans among them. Top each tortilla with one "egg" and top each, evenly, with sauce.

# Papa Chorizo Frittata

*Field Roast Mexican Chipotle Sausages are one of my favorite things in the world. If I were Oprah I'd list it as one of my favorite things every single year for life! The Papa Chorizo Frittata was created out of my love for this sausage, therefore I highly recommend using this brand over any other vegan chorizo sausage out there.*

Two 12.3-ounce packages extra-firm silken tofu

2 tablespoons nutritional yeast

3 tablespoons potato starch

½ teaspoon stone-ground mustard

1 teaspoon fine sea salt

¼ teaspoon turmeric

½ teaspoon onion powder

3 tablespoons canola oil

2 red potatoes, scrubbed and cut into ½-inch cubes

½ cup diced white onion

1 garlic clove, minced

One 3-ounce link vegan chorizo sausage

¼ cup chopped roasted red bell pepper

2 tablespoons chopped fresh parsley

Preheat the oven to 375°F. Grease a 9-inch springform pan with shortening or oil.

Put the tofu, nutritional yeast, potato starch, mustard, salt, turmeric, and onion powder into a blender and blend until smooth. Pour into a large bowl.

Crumble the chorizo sausage or pulse it in a food processor for about 30 seconds.

Warm the oil in a large skillet over medium to medium-high heat. Add the potatoes and onion and cook, stirring often, until the potatoes are tender, about 8 minutes. Add the garlic and chorizo and cook for an additional 2 to 3 minutes. Turn off the heat and stir in the bell pepper and parsley.

Stir the potato mixture into the tofu mixture. Pour into the prepared pan and bake for 35 to 45 minutes or until the filling is firm and a toothpick comes out clean.

Cool for 10 to 15 minutes. Remove the frittata from the pan and serve. This can be served warm, at room temperature, or cold.

# Flautas sin Pollo

Flauta *means "flute" in Spanish, and although these resemble tasty little instruments, I don't recommend you try to play them. But I do highly recommend eating them! My favorite part of these flautas is the marinated seitan. The first time I made these I ate half the seitan right out the oven before I remembered that I had to use it for this recipe. Luckily, one or two strips of seitan are usually left over when making these, so feel free to snack away if the mood hits you.*

1 cup chopped cilantro

6 garlic cloves

¼ cup plus 1 tablespoon canola oil, plus more for frying

2 chipotle peppers in adobo sauce

3 tablespoons fresh lime juice (about 2 small limes)

½ teaspoon fine sea salt

1 recipe Chik'n Seitan (page 258), cut into thin strips

1½ teaspoons dried oregano

1 green onion, chopped

2 cups cooked pinto beans

¼ cup vegetable stock

Twelve 6-inch flour or corn tortillas

Salsa

Preheat the oven to 375°F. Lightly oil a baking sheet or line it with nonstick aluminum foil.

Put the cilantro, 3 of the garlic cloves, the ¼ cup canola oil, and the chipotles, lime juice, and salt in a food processor and purée until smooth. Toss the seitan with this purée and marinate for at least 20 minutes.

Place the marinated seitan on the prepared baking sheet and bake for 15 to 20 minutes or until golden brown.

Heat the 1 tablespoon canola oil in a medium saucepan over medium heat. Mince the remaining 3 garlic cloves, then add the minced garlic, oregano, and green onion to the pan. Cook

134    

for 1 minute, stirring frequently. Add the beans and stock and cook just until the stock is absorbed. Remove from the heat.

Heat the tortillas, 3 at a time, in the microwave for 30 seconds to soften. Spoon 2 tablespoons of the pinto bean mixture into the center of each tortilla. Top with 1 to 2 seitan strips and tightly roll the tortilla around the filling. Repeat with the remaining tortillas, beans, and seitan.

Pour ½ inch of oil into a skillet. Fry 3 flautas at a time, starting seam side down, until crisp and golden brown, 2 to 3 minutes, turning often. Transfer to paper towels to drain. Serve with salsa.

## Cook's Tip

For more robust flavor, the seitan can be marinated overnight.

# Taco Soup

MAKES 4 TO 6 SERVINGS

*If you have my first cookbook,* Quick and Easy Vegan Comfort Food, *then you know tacos hold a special place in my heart. In fact, tacos were the first recipe I ever veganized and a meal that I have at least once a week. But why confine tacos to a soft or crunchy tortilla shell? That seems so restrictive. Taco Soup is everything great about tacos in a savory, hearty soup that will have you saying, "What taco shell?"*

3½ cups vegetable stock

1½ teaspoons hickory liquid smoke

1 cup textured vegetable protein (TVP)

2 tablespoons canola oil

½ medium white onion, diced

½ medium red or yellow bell pepper, diced

5 tablespoons Taco Seasoning (page 253)

2 cups cooked kidney beans

One 14-ounce can petite diced tomatoes, with juices

1 cup fresh or frozen corn

1 cup tomato sauce

### Cook's Tip

When reheating leftovers, be sure to add a little extra vegetable stock as the TVP will absorb some of the stock when stored.

Bring 1 cup of the stock and the liquid smoke to a boil in a small saucepan. Remove from the heat, stir in the TVP, and let sit for 5 minutes.

Warm the canola oil in a soup pot over medium heat. Add the onion and bell pepper and sauté until the onion is translucent, about 3 minutes. Stir in the rehydrated TVP and 2 tablespoons of the Taco Seasoning and cook for an additional 2 minutes.

Stir in the beans, tomatoes, corn, tomato sauce, the remaining 2½ cups vegetable stock and the remaining 3 tablespoons Taco Seasoning and cook until warmed through, about 10 minutes. Ladle into bowls and serve.

# Tempeh Soft Tacos with Lime Crema

*Fresh-Mex food has become the latest trend in Mexican cooking in the States. As the name implies, it uses fresh, simple, whole-food ingredients that are lower in fat than traditional Mexican food but still hold bold, rich flavors. These tacos are the ultimate in fresh-Mex cooking and pair well with a Classic Margarita (page 145).*

**MAKES 10 TACOS**

**LIME CREMA**

1 cup plain soy yogurt

Juice of 1 large lime

**TEMPEH SOFT TACOS**

3 tablespoons canola oil

½ small white onion, sliced thin

½ bell pepper, any color, sliced thin

2 garlic cloves, sliced thin

One 8-ounce package tempeh, any variety, sliced thin

1 chipotle pepper in adobo sauce, minced

1 teaspoon dried oregano

2 tablespoons Taco Seasoning (page 253)

½ cup vegetable stock

10 corn tortillas

**TO MAKE THE LIME CREMA:** Whisk together the yogurt and lime juice in a small bowl. Cover and refrigerate while you prepare the tacos.

**TO MAKE THE TACOS:** Warm 2 tablespoons of the canola oil in a skillet over medium heat. Add the onion, bell pepper, and garlic and sauté for 3 minutes. Add the remaining 1 tablespoon canola oil and the tempeh and sauté for 5 minutes or until the tempeh is lightly browned on both sides. Stir in the chipotle, oregano, Taco Seasoning, and stock and simmer until the liquid is absorbed, about 5 minutes.

Warm the tortillas, 3 at a time, in the microwave for 30 seconds. Fill with the tempeh mixture, then top with Lime Crema. Repeat until all the tortillas and tempeh are used.

# Quinoa-Stuffed Poblanos with Black Beans and Mango Peach Salsa

*Poblanos resemble oversized jalapeños, and for this reason I was afraid to cook with them for years. But, in fact, they're extremely mild peppers that roast up wonderfully and can be easily stuffed with your favorite filling. Here's my favorite filling of quinoa, black beans, and Mango Peach Salsa. Hopefully it will become yours, too.*

4 poblano peppers

2 tablespoons canola oil

½ cup diced white or yellow onion

3 garlic cloves, minced

1½ cups cooked black beans

1 teaspoon chili powder

¼ teaspoon ground cumin

1 cup vegetable stock

1 cup cooked quinoa (see page 23)

1 recipe Mango-Peach Salsa (recipe follows)

Preheat the oven to 450°F. Line a baking sheet with foil.

Place the poblanos on the baking sheet and brush with 1 tablespoon of the canola oil. Roast for 8 to 10 minutes or until the skin blisters and begins to darken.

Warm the remaining 1 tablespoon canola oil in a medium saucepan over medium heat. Add the onion and sauté for 2 minutes, then stir in the garlic and cook an additional minute. Add the beans, chili powder, cumin, and stock. Cook until the mixture begins to lightly boil. Cover and simmer on low heat for 5 minutes.

Remove the poblanos from the oven, cut open like you would a baked potato, and stuff each pepper equally with the quinoa, then the black beans. Top with the Mango Peach Salsa.

# Mango Peach Salsa

**MAKES 2 CUPS**

1 cup diced mangos

1 cup diced peaches

½ cup diced red onion

2 roma tomatoes, diced

¼ cup chopped cilantro

1 tablespoon fresh lime juice

Mix all the ingredients in a medium bowl. Cover with plastic wrap and refrigerate until ready to use.

## Cook's Tip

I am horrible at cutting mangoes, and when it comes to peeling peaches I would rather sit and watch paint dry. If you're like me, then go for the frozen version of each. They take about 30 minutes to defrost at room temperature, or you can defrost them in the microwave in about 30 seconds.

# Chipotle Black Bean Burgers

*Eating veggie burgers always feels like I'm eating junk food, but one can hardly classify burgers made of black beans and brown rice as junk food. One of the great joys of being vegan is eating great-tasting whole foods that not only taste phenomenal but are good for you. And these Chipotle Black Bean Burgers fit the bill.*

4 tablespoons canola oil

½ cup diced white or yellow onion

½ cup diced green bell pepper

2 garlic cloves, minced

3 cups cooked black beans

1 to 2 chipotle peppers in adobo sauce, chopped

1 teaspoon adobo sauce (from the can of chipotle peppers)

¾ cup cooked brown rice

½ teaspoon fine sea salt

1 teaspoon ground cumin

1 cup unseasoned bread crumbs

6 whole-grain or spelt hamburger buns

6 slices tomato

6 slices red onion

3 romaine lettuce leaves, cut in half

Ketchup

Warm 2 tablespoons of the oil in a small skillet over medium heat. Add the onion and bell pepper and sauté until tender, about 3 minutes. Add the garlic and sauté for an additional minute.

Put the onion mixture, black beans, chipotle peppers, adobo sauce, brown rice, salt, and cumin into a food processor and process until the black beans are mashed but some small pieces of black beans are still visible.

Transfer the mixture to a large bowl and fold in the bread crumbs.

Divide the mixture into 6 balls of similar size (about ½ cup each) and flatten into patties. Refrigerate for 15 minutes.

Warm the remaining 2 tablespoons of canola oil in a large frying pan or cast-iron skillet over medium heat. Cook the patties for 2 to 3 minutes on each side or until each side begins to darken, adding oil as needed.

Place each burger on a bun and dress with the tomatoes, onion, lettuce, and ketchup.

## Cook's Tip

If using canned beans, 3 cups is approximately two 15-ounce cans. Make sure to rinse the beans well before using.

# Chorizo Empanadas

*Empanadas are an amazing and versatile Mexican pastry that can be filled with savory fillings like crumbled chorizo or sweet fillings like cinnamon apple. Once you've played with this base recipe a few times, try venturing out with your own favorite spices and textures. You really can't go wrong.*

2½ cups unbleached all-purpose flour

¼ cup shortening

½ teaspoon fine sea salt

¾ cup cold water

Two 3-ounce vegan chorizo links

1 garlic clove

1 tablespoon canola oil, plus more for frying

½ cup diced red onion

½ small red bell pepper, chopped

Salsa

Pulse the flour, shortening, and salt in a food processor until pebbly. While the processor is running, slowly add up to ¾ cup cold water until a dough forms.

Turn the dough out into a medium bowl. Cover with plastic wrap and refrigerate while you make the filling.

Pulse the chorizo links and garlic in a food processor until the chorizo is crumbled. Set aside.

Warm the 1 tablespoon canola oil in a medium skillet over medium heat. Add the onion and bell pepper and sauté until the onion becomes translucent, about 3 minutes. Add the crumbled chorizo mixture and cook for an additional 3 minutes.

Preheat a deep fryer to 375°F or heat about ½ inch of oil in a large frying pan over medium heat. To test the heat, sprinkle a small drop of water into the oil. When the water begins to pop, the oil is ready.

142

Remove the dough from the refrigerator and place it on a lightly floured surface. Roll out the dough about ⅛ thick. Cut the dough into circles with a 3½-inch biscuit cutter or the mouth of an 8-ounce drinking glass. Place 1 tablespoon of chorizo mixture onto one side of the circle and fold the circle in half, pressing the ends closed with your fingertips. Crimp the outer edge shut with a fork to seal. Repeat until all the dough is used. You might have a little filling left over.

Fry the empanadas in small batches until golden brown on both sides, about 2 to 3 minutes. Drain on paper towels. Serve warm with salsa.

## Cook's Tip

**My favorite vegan chorizo is Field Roast Mexican Chipotle Sausage. It has the perfect blend of spices and a superb texture. If you use another brand, make sure that you only use 6 ounces of chorizo total.**

# Mexican Chocolate Mousse

**MAKES 4 SERVINGS**

*Mexican chocolate combines the creamy richness of chocolate with hints of cinnamon, vanilla, and almond. In my book that makes it the best chocolate ever invented. To be honest with you, this is more of a pudding than a mousse, but the word "pudding" is one of my least favorite words, so mousse it is!*

1 cup unsweetened coconut milk

12 ounces soft silken tofu

6 tablespoons unsweetened cocoa powder

¾ cup sugar

½ teaspoon vanilla extract

½ teaspoon ground cinnamon

¼ teaspoon almond extract

⅛ teaspoon xanthan gum

Pinch of cayenne pepper

Put all the ingredients in a food processor and process until smooth. Transfer to four 6-ounce ramekins and chill for at least 30 minutes. Serve cold.

# Classic Margarita

*What's a Cinco de Mayo party without the margaritas? Making a margarita is as easy as combining just four ingredients, and once you've had this version, you'll never buy premade margarita mix again.*

MAKES 10 MARGARITAS

2½ cups gold tequila

2½ cups fresh lime juice (about 20 limes)

1 cup agave nectar

3 tablespoons triple sec or Cointreau

Ice

Pour the tequila, lime juice, agave nectar, and triple sec into a large pitcher and stir to combine. Add enough ice to fill the pitcher and serve.

## Cook's Tip

A hand-held lime squeezer makes quick work of juicing limes and gets the maximum juice out of them with the least amount of effort (see page 27).

# Frozen Mango Margarita

MAKES 4 MARGARITAS

*I'm personally a fan of the Classic Margarita (page 145) on the rocks, but when I'm looking for a change of pace it's either this Frozen Mango Margarita or the Pineapple Margarita (below), hands down.*

1 pound frozen diced mango
¾ cup water
⅓ cup agave nectar
½ cup gold or white tequila
¼ cup triple sec
½ lime, juiced
1 cup ice

Put all the ingredients in a blender and blend until smooth.

# Pineapple Margarita

MAKES 4 MARGARITAS

*The quality of the pineapple juice really affects the taste of this margarita. Fresh pineapple juice is preferred as it is the sweetest and has the strongest pineapple flavor. If you use canned pineapple juice, make sure to taste it for sweetness before serving. You might need to add a tad bit more agave nectar.*

½ cup fresh lime juice (about 5 limes)
¾ cup white tequila
¼ cup triple sec
1½ cups pineapple juice
2 tablespoons agave nectar

Stir all the ingredients together in a pitcher and serve cold, over ice.

# ★ Independence Day ★

INDEPENDENCE DAY IS more than just a great sci-fi movie featuring Will Smith or an excuse to throw a big cookout. It's the day when the Declaration of Independence was signed, giving us freedom from British rule (but we still love the Brits!). Independence Day is also a federal holiday, which means almost everyone gets the day off. So, naturally, a three-day weekend of cookouts, fireworks, and parties is in order. This chapter has everything you need to start your Independence Day celebration off right.

BBQ Tempeh Hoagies with Chipotle Mayo

BBQ Baked Beans

Grilled Corn with Herbed Butter

Coleslaw

Potato Salad

Broccoli Salad

Patriotic Parfait

Pride Punch

Fresh-Squeezed Lemonade

# BBQ Tempeh Hoagies with Chipotle Mayo

**MAKES 4 HOAGIES**

*Get your napkins ready and your bib on tight because you're about to dive into a boat of Smokey Maple BBQ Sauce with a little tempeh on the side. If there are skeptics of vegan food in your life, then this is the hoagie to start them out on. I set these out at a cookout last year just for a moment while I went to grab some chips, and when I came back I found they had all been kidnapped by my omnivore friends. Let's see how long they last at your summer cookout.*

2 tablespoons canola oil

½ small white onion, sliced thin

½ medium bell pepper, any color, sliced thin

One 8-ounce package tempeh, any variety, sliced thin

1 cup Smokey Maple BBQ Sauce (page 256)

4 hoagie rolls, split and lightly toasted

### CHIPOTLE MAYO

½ cup vegan mayonnaise

1 teaspoon vegan Worcestershire sauce

1 chipotle pepper in adobo sauce

1 teaspoon adobo sauce (from the can of chipotle peppers)

¼ teaspoon dried oregano

Warm the canola oil in a medium skillet over medium heat. Add the onion and bell pepper and cook for 1 minute. Add the tempeh and cook for 4 to 5 minutes or until the tempeh is warmed through, stirring often.

While the tempeh is cooking, put all the chipotle mayo ingredients in a mini food processor and process until smooth.

Stir the Smokey Maple BBQ Sauce into the tempeh and cook until warmed through.

Spread some Chipotle Mayo on each side of the hoagie rolls and fill with the tempeh mixture.

# BBQ Baked Beans

*Okay, so I told a little fib. These beans aren't actually baked, but whipped up in one big pot on the stovetop. In only 30 minutes you have rich, smokey BBQ beans that will taste like you slaved away in the kitchen all day.*

1½ tablespoons canola oil

¾ cup diced white or Vidalia onions

4 garlic cloves, minced

2 cups ketchup

3 tablespoons white vinegar

6 tablespoons agave nectar

¼ cup vegan Worcestershire sauce

1½ teaspoons chili powder

¼ teaspoon dry mustard

¼ to ½ teaspoon red pepper flakes, depending on desired heat

5 cups cooked navy beans

Warm the canola oil in a medium saucepan over medium heat. Add the onions and sauté until translucent, about 3 minutes. Add the garlic and sauté until fragrant, about 1 minute.

Stir in the ketchup, vinegar, agave nectar, Worcestershire sauce, chili powder, mustard, and red pepper flakes.

Reduce the heat, cover, and simmer for 15 minutes. Stir in the beans and simmer, uncovered, for an additional 10 minutes.

# Grilled Corn with Herbed Butter

**MAKES 6 SERVINGS**

*If you don't have access to an outdoor or indoor grill, feel free to cheat and either steam or boil your corn. The herbed butter is the star of the show, so no matter how you prepare your corn it is sure to be delicious.*

¼ cup nonhydrogenated margarine, softened

1 garlic clove, minced

1 teaspoon minced fresh marjoram

1 teaspoon minced fresh thyme

⅛ teaspoon fine sea salt

6 ears fresh corn, husks on

Cream the margarine with the garlic, marjoram, thyme, and salt in a small bowl. Cover and refrigerate until ready to use.

Remove any loose husks from the corn and soak the corn in cool water for 5 minutes. Remove and shake off any excess water. Place the corn on a preheated indoor or outdoor grill (outdoor grills work the best). Brown the corn on all sides, turning every 5 to 10 minutes. It's okay if the husks begin to burn a little.

Remove the corn from the grill, gently peel back the husks, and slather with the herbed butter.

# Coleslaw

*Premade coleslaw mix is a quick, easy, and cheap alternative to shredding your own vegetables. Get the slaw mix with green cabbage, red cabbage, and carrots to get the most bang for your buck. The longer this sits the better it gets, so if your cookout is in the afternoon make this first thing in the morning or the night before.*

**MAKES 4 TO 6 SERVINGS**

1 pound premade coleslaw mix

⅔ cup vegan mayonnaise

6 tablespoons unsweetened rice or soy milk

2 tablespoons white vinegar

6 tablespoons sugar

½ teaspoon fine sea salt

Freshly ground black pepper

Stir together all the ingredients in a large bowl, cover with plastic wrap, and refrigerate for at least 2 hours.

# Potato Salad

*A cookout isn't a cookout without potato salad, at least in my humble opinion. I like to give my potato salad plenty of time to sit and let all the flavors meld. I highly recommend refrigerating it overnight if you have the time. But if you're short on time, it is still sure to be the hit of your cookout even with only 30 or 40 minutes in the fridge.*

1 pound russet or Yukon Gold potatoes, peeled and cut into ½-inch chunks

Pinch of fine sea salt

½ cup diced red onion

½ teaspoon yellow mustard

½ cup vegan mayonnaise

1 teaspoon sugar

6 tablespoons sweet pickle relish

1 celery rib, diced

Pinch of paprika

Place the potatoes in a medium stockpot with the salt and enough water to cover them by 1 inch. Boil until tender, about 20 minutes. Drain the potatoes and cool completely.

Mix the potatoes with the onion, mustard, mayonnaise, sugar, sweet relish, and celery in a large bowl. Transfer to a serving dish and sprinkle with the paprika. Serve cold.

# Broccoli Salad

Cookout food tends to be all about the starch. Between the Potato Salad (page 152), BBQ Tempeh Hoagies with Chipotle Mayo (page 148), and Grilled Corn with Herbed Butter (page 150) your guests will be satisfied, but to make it a complete meal you have to have some veggies. I like to infuse a little color into my cookouts by adding fresh broccoli to the mix with this sweet and crunchy broccoli salad.

**MAKES 6 TO 8 SERVINGS**

1½ pounds broccoli florets, chopped

¼ cup raw sunflower seeds

½ cup raisins

¼ cup diced white onion

½ cup unsalted cashew butter

¼ cup apple cider vinegar

2 tablespoons agave nectar

½ teaspoon Bragg Liquid Aminos

¾ cup plain rice milk

Mix the broccoli, sunflower seeds, raisins, and onion in a large bowl.

Whisk the cashew butter, vinegar, agave nectar, liquid aminos, and milk together in a small bowl. Pour over the broccoli mixture and stir to coat.

Cover and refrigerate for at least 1 hour. Serve chilled.

# Patriotic Parfait

**MAKES 4 SERVINGS**

### Cook's Tip

I like using a little bit of agar to fluff up the whipped cream a bit. If you'd like to try this option, simply simmer 1 teaspoon agar flakes with ⅓ cup water until the agar flakes are dissolved. Simmer on low heat for 5 minutes, then add to the tofu mixture before blending.

*Presentation is everything when it comes to parfaits. The natural colors of the fruits and whipped cream are what make this healthy dessert so beautiful, so accentuate these colors with the perfect serving cups. Vintage milkshake glasses are a favorite to layer these parfaits in, or try using large wine glasses for a more sophisticated feel.*

½ vanilla bean, split lengthwise

12.3 ounces firm or extra-firm silken tofu

⅓ cup Grade A maple syrup

1 tablespoon plain soy milk

2 tablespoons canola oil, optional

Pinch of fine sea salt

1 pound fresh strawberries, stemmed and sliced

1 pound fresh blueberries

Scrape the seeds out of the half vanilla bean with a spoon.

Put the tofu, maple syrup, milk, vanilla bean seeds, oil (if using), and salt into a food processor and blend until smooth. Refrigerate for at least 30 minutes. It is preferable to refrigerate this whipped cream overnight.

Divide the strawberry slices among 10- to 12-ounce serving glasses, then top with a few dollops of whipped cream. Top the whole thing off with fresh blueberries and serve.

# Pride Punch

10 Cane Rum is made of pure sugarcane and has a sweeter, smoother flavor than traditional rum. Mixed with a little pineapple juice, amaretto, and the light taste of mint, it makes a superb cocktail that adds a bit of coolness to a hot summer day.

2½ cups pineapple juice

1 cup 10 cane rum

½ cup amaretto

1 bunch mint, torn

Stir together all the ingredients in a large pitcher or punch bowl. Serve over ice.

## Cook's Tip

To bring out the flavor of the mint, once it's torn, rub it between your fingers to release its natural oils before adding it to your Pride Punch.

# Fresh-Squeezed Lemonade

**MAKES 5 CUPS**

*There's something about a pitcher of fresh lemonade sitting out on the counter waiting to be poured that just screams summer to me. I couldn't imagine a cookout without it, and I could never imagine making it from concentrate or getting that store-bought stuff. Making 5 cups of lemonade is as easy as juicing four big lemons and stirring in a little sugar and water. It doesn't get much easier than that.*

> 1 cup fresh lemon juice (about 4 large lemons)
> 4 cups cold water
> ¾ cup sugar

Stir all the ingredients together in a 2-quart pitcher until the sugar dissolves. Serve over ice.

# ★ Halloween ★

THE SUZY HOMEMAKER in me emerges when Halloween comes around. I go wild decorating the house with fake cobwebs and spiders, ghosts and goblins, and, of course, jack-o'-lanterns everywhere you look. Most importantly, I love handing out treats to the neighborhood children and reliving the fun-filled Halloween nights of my youth through them.

Most people don't realize the bevy of vegan candy that is available at any grocery store. Here's just a short list of the vegan options out there:

Airheads Taffy

Atkins peanut butter bars

Atomic Fireballs

Bottle Caps

Brach's Cinnamon Hard Candy

Charms Blow Pops

Charms lollipops (without gum)

Chick-O-Stick

Cracker Jack

Cry Baby

Dots

Dum Dum Pops

FruitaBü

Gobstoppers

Goldenberg's Peanut Chews

Hot Tamales

Hubba Bubba bubble gum

Jolly Rancher lollipops and hard candies

Jujubes

Jujyfruits

Lemonheads

Life Savers

Mambas

Mary Janes (regular and Peanut Butter Kisses)

Mike and Ike

Nerds

Now and Later

Pez

Red Vines (American Licorice Co.)

Ring Pop lollipops

Runts

Skittles

Smarties

Sour Patch Kids

Super Bubble

Super Ropes (American Licorice Co.)

Swedish Fish

Sweet Tarts

Tropical Source mini chocolate bags

Twizzlers

Zotz

Giving away candy at Halloween is fun, but whipping up your own homemade ghoulish concoctions brings the holiday to life. Now that you've got your Halloween candy, it's time to create these homemade treats.

Pumpkin Casserole
Severed Fingers
Ghost Sandwiches
Mummy Mini Pizzas
Orange-o'-Lanterns
Eyeball Cake Pops
Dirt and Worm Cupcakes
Candy Corn on a Stick
Marzipan Candy Corn
Marzipan Pumpkins

# Pumpkin Casserole

This pumpkin casserole isn't exactly a casserole with pumpkin in it, it's a pumpkin filled with casserole! Yes, Halloween is all about the sweets and treats, but you've got to have some real food, too, and what better way to serve it up than in a hollowed-out pumpkin? The closer it gets to Halloween, the cheaper pumpkins are, so if you can wait to make this on Halloween day you'll get a super-cheap pumpkin and a fun and delicious dinner.

1 medium pumpkin (about 8 to 10 pounds)

¼ cup nonhydrogenated margarine

½ cup diced white onion

¼ cup unbleached all-purpose flour

3½ cups plain oat milk or soy milk

1¼ teaspoons fine sea salt

¼ teaspoon ground black pepper

1½ cups frozen peas

1½ cups cooked chickpeas

2 cups Cheezly mature white cheddar, shredded

One 12-ounce package penne pasta, cooked according to package directions

### Cook's Tip

Make sure to bake the pumpkin for only 15 minutes. The pumpkin in this dish is used in place of a casserole dish and is not eaten. If you cook it too long, the pumpkin will get soft and will be a bit harder to work with when transferring from the oven to your dinner table.

Cut the top of the pumpkin off, leaving a 4- to 5-inch opening. Scoop out the seeds and pulp.

Preheat the oven to 350°F. Line a baking sheet with foil.

Melt the margarine in a medium saucepan over medium heat, add the onion, and sauté until tender, 2 to 3 minutes.

Stir in the flour. Add the milk, salt, and pepper. Cook, stirring frequently, until the sauce begins to thicken and bubble. Add the peas, chickpeas, 1 cup of the cheddar, and the pasta.

Mix thoroughly until the sauce evenly covers the pasta. Spoon the pasta into the prepared pumpkin, then sprinkle with the remaining 1 cup cheddar. Bake for 15 minutes.

# Severed Fingers

**MAKES 8 FINGERS**

*Presentation is everything when it comes to making your holiday dishes ghoulish and frightening. This recipe is so quick and easy, it's insane. Quick recipes like this give you plenty of time to decorate your house and get it ready for a holiday party that your neighbors will envy.*

8 vegan hot dogs
8 slivered almonds or green pumpkin seeds
Ketchup

Cook the hot dogs according to the package directions and allow to cool enough to handle.

Stick an almond slice or pumpkin seed into one end of each hot dog, creating a fingernail. Arrange the fingers on a serving plate and cover the ends without fingernails with ketchup.

# Ghost Sandwiches

*Around the Halloween season inexpensive sets of Halloween-themed cookie cutters are at nearly every neighborhood home store. Don't feel confined to just using the ghost-shaped cookie cutters—you can create tombstone, jack-o'-lantern, and bat sandwiches as well. Let your imagination run free.*

**MAKES 8 SANDWICHES**

8 slices white bread

½ cup vegan cream cheese

1 tablespoon confectioners' sugar

24 dried currants, sweetened cranberries, or raisins

Lightly toast the bread. Cut each slice into a ghost shape with a paring knife or a gingerbread-girl cookie cutter.

Stir together the cream cheese and confectioners' sugar and spread evenly on the toast.

Use the currants for eyes and mouths.

# Mummy Mini Pizzas

**MAKES 12 PIZZAS**

### Cook's Tip

Usually you want gooey melted cheese on a pizza, but for these pizzas keeping the strips of cheese distinct helps them look more like mummy wrappings. Vegan cheese doesn't have a reputation for melting quickly, but just in case yours decides to go rogue, check on your mini pizzas around the 7- to 8-minute mark to make sure your cheese strips are still intact.

*A mummy isn't a mummy without his wrappings on just right. Forgo the typical shredded cheese you usually use on pizza. Instead, grab a block of vegan mozzarella and create long thin strips with a cheese cutter or paring knife. Cheezly brand tends to be the sturdiest for this task.*

6 English muffins
¾ cup Pizza Sauce (page 257)
One 3.5-ounce package vegan mozzarella, sliced into long thin strips
8 black olives, sliced into ¼-inch disks

Preheat the oven to 400°F (or 350°F if using a toaster oven).

Split the English muffins in half. Spread 1 tablespoon of Pizza Sauce on each half.

Lay strips of cheese across the muffin for the mummy's wrappings and place olive slices near the top of the pizza as eyes.

Place the mummies on a baking sheet and bake for about 10 minutes or until the cheese is melted and the muffin is toasty.

# Orange-o'-Lanterns

*Halloween seems to be filled with nothing but candy and sweet treats. Take a break from the norm with these Orange-o'-Lanterns. They are a fun addition to any lunch box.*

**MAKES 4 SERVINGS**

4 large oranges

Just as you would a traditional jack-o'-lantern, carve small facial features in one side of each orange with a paring knife.

# Eyeball Cake Pops

*Getting perfectly round donut holes is key to the presentation of these Eyeball Cake Pops. This recipe purposefully calls for more dough than you'll need so you can practice getting the best donut holes possible. The great part is, just because your donut holes don't look perfect doesn't mean they don't taste perfect— so you can gobble up any mistakes. (In this recipe, each eyeball gets decorated, and then eaten, on a "stick." I suggest forks—so make sure you have a lot of forks!)*

1 tablespoon canola oil, plus more for frying

1 cup plus 2 tablespoons unbleached all-purpose flour

¾ teaspoon baking powder

¼ teaspoon baking soda

¼ teaspoon ground cinnamon

⅛ teaspoon ground nutmeg

¼ teaspoon fine sea salt

¼ cup granulated sugar

2 tablespoons light brown sugar

¾ teaspoon Ener-G Egg Replacer

1 tablespoon water

2 tablespoons plain soy yogurt

2 tablespoons plain almond, rice, oat, or soy milk

½ cup unsweetened applesauce

Preheat a deep fryer to 350°F or heat about ½ inch of oil in a large frying pan over medium heat. To test the heat, sprinkle a small drop of water into the oil. When the water begins to pop, the oil is ready.

Stir together the flour, baking powder, baking soda, cinnamon, nutmeg, salt, granulated sugar, and brown sugar in a large bowl.

Whisk the egg replacer with water in a small bowl, then whisk in the yogurt, 1 tablespoon oil, and the milk and applesauce.

Pour the yogurt mixture into flour mixture and stir to combine. Drop rounded teaspoons of dough into the hot oil and fry in small batches for 1 to 2 minutes or until light, fluffy, and golden. Drain on paper towels.

## Decoration

1 cup vegan white chocolate chips
24 vegan semisweet chocolate chips
Red decorating frosting

Melt the white chocolate chips over low heat in a double boiler, and keep the chocolate warm while you work. If you don't have a double boiler, put the white chocolate chips into a microwave-safe bowl and microwave on high power for 1 minute, stirring halfway through, or until melted.

With a fork, spear each donut hole and submerge it in the melted white chocolate to coat it, then gently tap off any excess.

Stick a semisweet chocolate chip onto each dipped donut hole. Place the forks (handle down) in a mug and allow the chocolate coating to harden.

Once the chocolate has hardened, use the red decorating frosting to add squiggly veins radiating out from the chocolate chip pupils.

> ### Cook's Tip
>
> To make homemade red frosting, cut the Cream Cheeze Frosting recipe (page 246) in half and add a few drops of red food coloring or beet juice. Fill a pastry bag with frosting and use the fine tip to decorate.

# Dirt and Worm Cupcakes

*These cupcakes are decorated with little mini mounds of cookie dirt and crispy white chocolate–coated worms. The key to making the baking and assembly process as quick and easy as possible is multitasking. While the cupcakes are cooking, prepare the Chocolate Cream Cheeze Frosting as well as the worms. By the time the cupcakes are baked and cooled, you'll have all the components ready to assemble your cupcakes.*

¾ cup nonhydrogenated margarine, softened

¼ cup unsweetened applesauce

¼ cup plain soy yogurt

1 tablespoon apple cider vinegar

¾ cup unsweetened cocoa powder

2 cups sugar

1 teaspoon baking soda

2 teaspoons baking powder

½ teaspoon fine sea salt

1 teaspoon vanilla extract

2 cups unbleached all-purpose flour

1½ cups plain rice, almond, soy, or oat milk

1 recipe Chocolate Cream Cheeze Frosting (page 246)

Preheat the oven to 350°F. Line two 12-cup cupcake tins with paper baking cups.

Cream the margarine, applesauce, and yogurt in a large bowl with an electric mixer. Add the vinegar, cocoa powder, and sugar and beat until smooth. Beat in the baking soda, baking powder, salt, and vanilla.

Add a heaping ½ cup of the flour, beating well on low speed, then about ½ cup of the milk, beating well. Repeat until all the flour and milk are incorporated. Pour the batter into the cupcake tins, filling each cup approximately one-half full.

Bake one pan at a time for 25 to 30 minutes or until a toothpick comes out clean. Cool completely before frosting with Chocolate Cream Cheeze Frosting.

## ⭐ Dirt and Worms

½ cup vegan white chocolate chips

1 tablespoon agave nectar

1 tablespoon warm water

1 cup chow mein noodles

12 Oreo cookies, crushed into crumbs

Melt the white chocolate chips in a microwave for 1 minute and stir until smooth.

Stir in the agave nectar and warm water, then gently fold in the chow mein noodles, stirring until they are coated.

Scoop the chow mein mixture onto wax paper and separate the noodles into individual worms as well as a few small clumps of worms. Allow the chocolate to completely set, 10 to 15 minutes.

Sprinkle the cupcakes with the Oreo cookie crumbs and gently press them into the frosting. When the worms are ready, arrange them on top of the cupcakes.

# Candy Corn on a Stick

MAKES 12 POPSICLES

## Cook's Tip

If making a fresh batch of Vanilla Bean Ice Cream, follow the recipe through whisking in the vanilla seeds, then add the liquid mixture to the ice pop mold. If using Vanilla Bean Ice Cream that has already been frozen, allow it to soften before adding to the mold.

*Forget traditional candy corn full of high-fructose corn syrup, gelatin, and egg whites. Try these sweet and tangy candy corn ice pops. They're a healthy and easy way to remix the traditional candy corn, and kids absolutely love them.*

Orange juice
1 recipe Vanilla Bean Ice Cream (page 243), softened
Yellow food coloring, optional
1 recipe Fresh-Squeezed Lemonade (page 156)
12 popsicle sticks, if not included with your ice pop mold

Fill an ice pop mold one-third with orange juice and freeze for about 30 minutes or until the orange juice begins to harden.

Top with Vanilla Bean Ice Cream, filling the ice pop mold another third. Freeze for an additional 30 minutes or until the ice cream begins to harden.

Optionally, add a couple drops of yellow food coloring to your lemonade to brighten it up.

Finally, fill the last third of the ice pop mold with lemonade. Place the sticks in the ice pops and freeze for 4 hours or overnight.

# Marzipan Candy Corn

*Sadly, traditional candy corn is not vegan, but making your own vegan version at home using marzipan is ridiculously easy. Marzipan is a sweet almond confection that seems ultra-fancy and hard to use or work with. In reality, it is one of the simplest forms of candy making you'll ever do, mostly because 90 percent of the work is done for you. You can buy a 7-ounce roll of marzipan at just about any grocery store for a great price.*

MAKES ½ POUND

One 7-ounce package marzipan
Red and yellow food coloring
Confectioners' sugar

Divide the marzipan into 3 balls.

Add 4 to 5 drops of yellow food coloring to one of the balls and knead the color into it until it has a uniform bright yellow color.

Add 2 drops of red food coloring and 3 drops of yellow food coloring to the second ball of marzipan to produce an orange coloring. Knead the color into it until it is a uniform orange color, adding more food coloring as needed.

Lightly dust a work surface with confectioners' sugar. Roll the yellow marzipan ball into a long thin rope about ¼ inch thick. Repeat this process with the white and orange balls of marzipan. Ultimately each rope should be the same length and width.

Lie the three ropes side by side and tightly press them together. If the marzipan is no longer sticky, brush it with a little water to moisten it up a bit.

Very gently run a rolling pin over the tricolored marzipan strip to flatten the top and press it closer together.

Cut triangles out of the marzipan strip. Unlike traditional candy corn, some pieces will be white tipped and some will be yellow tipped. If the knife starts sticking, lightly dust it with confectioners' sugar between cuts.

# Marzipan Pumpkins

*These sweet almond Marzipan Pumpkins are super quick and easy to make—no artistic ability is required. If you can roll dough into a ball, then you can make homemade Marzipan Pumpkins that will make you look like an authentic candy craftsman.*

One 7-ounce package marzipan
Yellow food coloring
Red food coloring or beet juice
1 thyme sprig

Knead the marzipan until it becomes soft and pliable. Knead a small amount of yellow food coloring into the marzipan, then red, until you get a nice orange pumpkin color.

Form the dough into walnut-size balls. Make a small indentation at the top of each ball with your pinky finger.

Gently slide a toothpick from the tiny indentation at the top of the ball to the bottom, forming creases along the ball so that it resembles a pumpkin.

Add a thyme leaf to the top of each pumpkin as the stem and you're done!

# ★ Thanksgiving ★

CANADA AND THE United States might celebrate Thanksgiving on separate dates, but both holidays typically have one thing in common—turkey. Thanksgiving has become so much about the turkey that around this time of year you'll often hear "Happy Turkey Day!" used synonymously with "Happy Thanksgiving."

I have to admit, one of my favorite traditions on Thanksgiving is sitting down to a bountiful feast with a turkey at the table, front and center. Well, a picture of a turkey that is. You can sponsor your very own turkey from the Farm Sanctuary so that you, too, can be joined at the Thanksgiving dinner table by a lovely picture of the life you have helped save and enrich. Through its Adopt-A-Turkey project, the Farm Sanctuary has been able to save over one thousand turkeys thus far, and all it takes is a $25 donation to help. Head to www.adoptaturkey. org for more information and to adopt a turkey this Thanksgiving.

Tourkey Cutlets
Classic Macaroni and Cheeze
Corn Bread Stuffing
Southern-Style Greens
Roasted Root and Gourd Soup
Roasted Garlic Smashed Potatoes
Cranberry Sauce
Pumpkin Gingerbread with Pumpkin Butter
Raw Sweet Potato Pie
Pumpkin Pie Ice Cream

# Tourkey Cutlets

*I've been meat free for over eight Thanksgivings and have managed to make it through all of them without ever once eating Tofurky. When it comes to a big holiday meal, I like to make the traditional side dishes my main attractions and pile them high on the plate with a Tourkey Cutlet and Sage Gravy (page 248) as my side. Most importantly, I like my Thanksgiving dinner to be 100 percent homemade from top to bottom, and these cutlets are a simple way to make that possible. Tourkey Cutlets can be made up to three days before the holidays and panfried the day of.*

½ cup vital wheat gluten

¼ cup soy flour

3 cups water

3 tablespoons nutritional yeast

2 tablespoons Bragg Liquid Aminos

1 tablespoon vegan Worcestershire sauce

1 teaspoon onion powder

½ teaspoon dried sage (not ground)

½ teaspoon dried thyme

¼ teaspoon dried marjoram

3 tablespoons canola oil

Unbleached all-purpose flour for dusting the cutlets

1 recipe Sage Gravy (page 248)

Mix the vital wheat gluten and soy flour in a small bowl, then add ½ cup of the water and stir until it forms a ball.

On a lightly floured surface, knead the dough for a little less than 1 minute, then flatten to ¼-inch thickness and cut into 4 cutlets.

Put the remaining 2½ cups water and the nutritional yeast, liquid aminos, Worcestershire sauce, onion powder, sage, thyme, and marjoram in a medium saucepan and bring to a boil. Add the cutlets one piece at a time, being careful not to splash the hot broth.

Reduce the heat, cover, and simmer for 50 to 55 minutes or until all the broth has absorbed, stirring every 10 minutes.

Warm the canola oil in a skillet over medium-high heat until hot but not smoking. Dust the cutlets with flour and sear until lightly browned on each side, 1 to 2 minutes per side. Serve with Sage Gravy.

# Classic Macaroni and Cheeze

MAKES 6 TO 8 SERVINGS

*This was the hands-down favorite from my first book,* QUICK AND EASY VEGAN COMFORT FOOD. *I serve it at almost all my holiday parties. No doubt it will fall into heavy rotation at yours.*

1 pound macaroni or rotini

2 medium Yukon Gold potatoes, peeled and diced

1 medium carrot, peeled and diced

⅔ cup diced white or yellow onions

2½ cups water

⅔ cup canola oil

⅓ cup raw cashews

⅓ cup raw macadamia nuts

2 teaspoons fine sea salt

2 garlic cloves, chopped

¼ teaspoon dry mustard

2 tablespoons fresh lemon juice

½ teaspoon ground black pepper

¼ teaspoon cayenne pepper

¼ cup unseasoned bread crumbs, optional

Preheat the oven to 350°F. Prepare the pasta according to the package directions. Drain and set aside.

While the pasta is cooking, combine the potatoes, carrot, onions, and water in a small saucepan over medium heat. Bring to a boil, then reduce the heat, cover, and simmer for 10 minutes or until the vegetables are tender. (The smaller you cut them, the less time it will take.)

Put the canola oil, cashews, macadamia nuts, salt, garlic, mustard, lemon juice, black pepper, cayenne, and the vegetables and their cooking water into a blender and process until completely smooth.

Toss the cooked pasta with the sauce until completely coated. Transfer to a lightly oiled 3-quart casserole dish or place 6 lightly oiled 6-ounce ramekins on a baking sheet and divide the mixture evenly among them. Sprinkle with the bread crumbs, if using. Bake for 30 minutes or until bubbling.

## Cook's Tip

If you do not have a high-speed blender, substitute more cashews for the macadamia nuts, as they are softer and easier to process.

# Corn Bread Stuffing

MAKES 12 SERVINGS

*My mother always made huge pans of stuffing, big enough to feed at least twelve people even though there were only four of us in the family. For this reason I know no other way of making stuffing than to make a pan big enough to feed an army. The great thing is that this stuffing gets even better with time and makes amazing leftovers, and, let's admit it, one of the best things about the day after Thanksgiving is eating leftovers all day long.*

1 cup cornmeal

1 cup unbleached all-purpose flour

2 tablespoons sugar

4 teaspoons baking powder

¾ teaspoon fine sea salt

2 teaspoons poultry seasoning

2 tablespoons dried sage (not ground)

¼ cup canola oil

2 tablespoons white vinegar

1¼ cups plain oat, rice, or soy milk

2 tablespoons nonhydrogenated margarine

3 celery ribs, diced

1 cup diced white onions

Freshly ground black pepper to taste

1 cup vegetable stock

Preheat the oven to 425°F. Oil a cast-iron skillet or 1½-quart casserole dish.

Mix the cornmeal, flour, sugar, baking powder, salt, poultry seasoning, and sage together until thoroughly combined. Make a well in the center and pour in the oil, vinegar, and milk. Mix until there are no lumps left, then transfer to the prepared pan.

Bake for 20 to 23 minutes or until a toothpick comes out clean.

While the corn bread is baking, melt the margarine in a small skillet. Add the celery and onion and sauté for 3 minutes or until the onions are translucent. Transfer to a large bowl.

Crumble the corn bread into the onion mixture and season with pepper. Transfer to a 2- or 3-quart casserole dish and pour the stock over the mixture. Cover with foil and bake for 10 minutes.

# Southern-Style Greens

There is one universal dish that is on the stovetop of every person I know on Thanksgiving, and that's greens. Usually they are cooked with some type of meat and simmered on the stovetop for hours. But this quick and easy vegan version is done in just 30 minutes without cooking in cruelty.

1 pound collard greens

½ pound kale

1 tablespoon canola oil

5 garlic cloves, minced

5 cups vegetable stock

1 teaspoon red pepper flakes

1 tablespoon hickory liquid smoke

Roll the leaves of the collard greens and chop into ½-inch strips. Repeat for the kale.

Warm the canola oil in a large soup pot over medium heat. Add the garlic and sauté until fragrant, about 1 minute, making sure the garlic doesn't burn. Add the stock, red pepper flakes, liquid smoke, collards, and kale and bring to a boil. Reduce the heat, cover, and simmer for 30 to 35 minutes or until the greens are tender.

# Roasted Root and Gourd Soup

**MAKES 6 TO 8 SERVINGS**

There's this great little urban farm in East Point, Georgia, called Truly Living Well that has incredible organic produce. In the fall they have baskets brimming with fresh-picked root vegetables and gourds just begging to be given a home in your belly. Butternut squash had always seemed like an intimidating vegetable to me, but then I discovered that once it's roasted it is incredibly easy to work with. It has a subtly sweet flavor that is only enhanced by the carrot and sweet potatoes in this soup. Treat this as a base recipe and play around with it as you like. If you're looking for a more savory soup, leave out the brown sugar; if you like a little more ginger, feel free to kick it up a notch. Allspice and cinnamon are also great additions if you're feeling really adventurous.

1 large butternut squash (about 3 pounds), halved and seeded

2 medium garnet sweet potatoes or yams, halved (1¾ to 2 pounds)

2 medium carrots, peeled and quartered lengthwise

1 tablespoon canola oil

1½ cups plain rice milk

2 cups vegetable stock

¼ cup loosely packed light brown sugar

¼ teaspoon ground ginger

½ teaspoon ground nutmeg

Preheat the oven to 400°F. Line a baking sheet with nonstick aluminum foil.

Arrange the squash, sweet potatoes, and carrots flesh side up on the prepared baking sheet. Lightly brush the canola oil over the vegetables. Roast for 45 to 55 minutes or until fork-tender. Carrots might be done earlier, so start checking on them at around 20 minutes.

Once the vegetables are roasted, scoop the flesh out of one half of the butternut squash. Put the squash, along with 1 carrot and 1 sweet potato, into the blender. Purée with ¾ cup of the milk until smooth, then transfer to a medium saucepan or Dutch oven. Repeat with the remaining vegetables and milk.

Stir in the stock, sugar, ginger, and nutmeg. Cook over medium heat until just warm, about 10 minutes. Ladle into serving bowls and enjoy!

# Roasted Garlic Smashed Potatoes

*There are two types of people in the world: those who hate garlic and those who put it in every dish they possibly can. Just in case you haven't noticed yet, I'm on the side of those who put it in every dish possible. Roasted garlic has a milder, sweeter flavor than raw garlic. For you true garlic lovers, two heads of roasted garlic might not be enough. Feel free to roast up a couple extra heads of garlic to add as you like.*

2 heads garlic

1 tablespoon plus 2 teaspoons extra-virgin olive oil

2 pounds russet potatoes (about 4 medium potatoes), scrubbed and cut into uniform chunks

Fine sea salt

¾ cup unsweetened soy or rice milk

Freshly ground black pepper to taste

Preheat the oven to 400°F.

Peel away the outer layers of the garlic bulb skin, leaving the skins of the individual cloves intact. Cut ¼ to ½ inch off the top of the bulb, exposing the top of the individual cloves of garlic.

Place the garlic heads in a baking pan and drizzle the 2 teaspoons olive oil over them, using your fingers to make sure each is well coated. Cover with aluminum foil. Bake for 30 to 35 minutes or until the cloves feel soft when pressed.

While the garlic is baking, put the potatoes in a medium saucepan with a pinch of salt and enough water to cover them by 1 inch. Bring to a boil over medium-high heat, cover, and boil until fork-tender, about 15 minutes.

When the garlic is cool enough to touch without burning yourself, use a paring knife to cut the skin slightly around each clove. Use a cocktail fork or your fingers to pull or squeeze the roasted garlic cloves out of their skins.

Drain the potatoes and transfer to a large bowl. Add the milk, the 1 tablespoon olive oil, and the roasted garlic cloves. Mash with a potato masher until you have your desired consistency. Season with salt and freshly ground pepper. Serve warm.

# Cranberry Sauce

**MAKES 4 TO 6 SERVINGS**

*Cranberry sauce is a great example of how quick and easy it is to cook from scratch. Once you try this sauce, you'll never buy that canned stuff again. If you prefer a smooth cranberry sauce, simply purée the sauce once it's cooled.*

One 10-ounce package fresh or frozen cranberries
½ cup sugar
⅓ cup orange juice
⅔ cup water

Mix all the ingredients together in a 2-quart saucepan over medium-high heat. Bring to a boil, stirring occasionally. Reduce the heat to medium or medium-low, cover, and simmer for 10 minutes, stirring occasionally.

Uncover and cook for an additional 10 minutes. Remove from the heat and allow to cool. As the sauce cools, it will thicken.

# Pumpkin Gingerbread with Pumpkin Butter

*The smell of pumpkin gingerbread baking in the oven and pumpkin butter warming on the stove is the best way to welcome your guests into your home for Thanksgiving. I always make pumpkin gingerbread the last step of my holiday meal so that when my friends and family come over, they immediately know they're in for some good eating.*

**MAKES 6 TO 8 SERVINGS**

1 cup unbleached all-purpose flour

1 cup whole wheat pastry flour

2 teaspoons baking soda

1 tablespoon baking powder

1 teaspoon ground cinnamon

1 teaspoon ground ginger

½ teaspoon fine sea salt

1 cup granulated sugar

½ cup loosely packed light brown sugar

1 cup pumpkin purée

½ cup canola oil

½ cup plain oat or rice milk

1 recipe Pumpkin Butter (recipe follows)

Preheat the oven to 350°F. Grease a 9-inch cake pan or spring-form pan with shortening or canola oil.

Mix the all-purpose flour, whole wheat pastry flour, baking soda, baking powder, cinnamon, ginger, and salt in a medium bowl.

Whisk the granulated sugar, brown sugar, pumpkin purée, and canola oil, then stir in the milk. Beat in the flour mixture with an electric mixer.

Pour the batter into the prepared ban. Bake for 40 to 45 minutes or until a toothpick comes out clean. Cool in the pan and then invert onto a serving tray. Serve the gingerbread warm or at room temperature, with Pumpkin Butter.

# ⭐Pumpkin Butter

**MAKES 2 CUPS**

One 15-ounce can pumpkin purée

1 cup unsweetened applesauce

½ cup loosely packed light brown sugar

¾ teaspoon ground cinnamon

⅛ teaspoon ground nutmeg

¼ teaspoon ground ginger

2 tablespoons orange juice

Mix the pumpkin, applesauce, sugar, cinnamon, nutmeg, and ginger in a small saucepan over medium heat.

Cook, uncovered, for 15 minutes, then reduce the heat to medium-low and cook for 40 minutes, stirring occasionally.

Remove from the heat and stir in the orange juice. Let cool, then store in an airtight container in the refrigerator until ready to use. This will keep in the refrigerator for 1 week.

# Raw Sweet Potato Pie

*Thanksgivings in my home aren't complete without the sweet potato pie. Traditionally I make a cooked sweet potato pie that takes only seconds to prepare but almost 1 hour to bake. Raw Sweet Potato Pie only takes minutes to make and is actually good for you. So this year when you get ready to cut that second slice of pie, don't feel guilty—you're actually eating a healthy, wholesome dish.*

**MAKES 6 TO 8 SERVINGS**

2 cups raw almonds

¼ teaspoon fine sea salt

1 cup Medjool dates (about 10 dates), pitted

4 cups raw garnet sweet potatoes or yams, peeled and cut into ½-inch cubes

½ avocado

¼ cup agave nectar

1 teaspoon ground cinnamon

¾ teaspoon ground nutmeg

Grind the almonds and salt in a food processor until you have a coarse meal. Sprinkle ¼ cup of almond meal on the bottom of a pie plate. Add the dates to the remaining almond meal in the food processor and pulse until well mixed and the dates are broken down. Press this mixture into the bottom and sides of the pie plate.

Put the sweet potato, avocado, agave nectar, cinnamon, and nutmeg in a high-speed blender or food processor and process until smooth. Spoon out into the crust. Allow to set in the refrigerator for at least 2 hours.

## Cook's Tip

The pie filling should be smooth and velvety, so if you don't have a high-speed blender you'll need a good-quality food processor to get the desired texture. Depending on the size of your food processor, you might need to process the filling in two small batches instead of one big one.

# Pumpkin Pie Ice Cream

MAKES 1 QUART

*The weather outside might be a little chilly, but your heart will warm with just one spoonful of this sinfully decadent pumpkin pie ice cream. This ice cream literally makes me do a little involuntary dance of joy every time I eat it. Like fresh pumpkin pie, Pumpkin Pie Ice Cream is best when eaten immediately after freezing. Put this ice cream in the ice cream maker just as you're about to sit down to dinner, and by the time you're done, dessert will be waiting for you.*

Two 12.3-ounce packages soft silken tofu

¾ cup pumpkin purée

¼ teaspoon ground allspice

½ teaspoon ground nutmeg

½ teaspoon ground cinnamon

½ teaspoon vanilla extract

½ cup loosely packed light brown sugar

¾ cup granulated sugar

Whisk together all the ingredients in a medium bowl until smooth, or blend them in a blender until smooth. Pour into an electric ice cream maker and freeze according to the manufacturer's directions. This usually takes 25 to 30 minutes to freeze.

# ★ Hanukkah ★

As a little African-American girl who celebrates Christmas, I used to be so jealous of my Jewish friends who got gifts for not one but eight days! My parents tried to teach me the meaning of Christmas and my friends' parents tried to teach them the significance of Hanukkah—but when you're 6 years old all you really care about is gifts, and the more the merrier. However, as I grew up, I came to understand that Hanukkah is not just an exciting time of year when gifts flow freely for eight days, but an important religious tradition dating back to the second century BC.

The eight-day "Festival of Lights" known as Hanukkah is a Jewish holiday that celebrates the rededication of the Holy Temple in Jerusalem at the time of the Maccabean Revolt. Around the world, every Hanukkah feast is different, but there are a few universal customs, one of which is fried foods. Fried foods are symbolic of the temple oil that was only supposed to last one day but miraculously lasted eight.

Not all Hanukkah recipes are quick, but they are very easy. Allowing the yeast to rise in the dough for the traditional Challah and Sufganiyot takes some time, but the sweet, soft, and flaky dough is worth it. If you're in a rush, there are three types of Latkes to please your palate, Portobello Brisket and Roasted Vegetables to make your stomach do a dance of joy, and my favorite fried dough—Applesauce Donut Holes. Happy Hanukkah!

Portobello Brisket

Roasted Vegetables

Potato Latkes

Sweet Potato and Parsnip Latkes

Cauliflower Latkes

Challah

Sufganiyot

Baked Sufganiyot

Applesauce Donut Holes

# Portobello Brisket

MAKES 4 SERVINGS

*Brisket is the centerpiece of every good Hanukkah feast. The key to this brisket is the marinating time. You can marinate it for as little as 20 minutes, but the flavor gets richer and richer as it marinates. The marinade takes only minutes to put together, so I like to throw all the ingredients in a gallon-size resealable plastic bag in the morning and then cook in the evening.*

4 portobello mushroom caps (about 1 pound)

1 small shallot, sliced thin

2 garlic cloves, minced

⅔ cup red wine

¼ cup Bragg Liquid Aminos

¼ cup Dijon mustard

⅓ cup canola oil

1½ teaspoons dried tarragon

Place the portobellos in a gallon-size resealable plastic bag. Add the shallot, garlic, wine, liquid aminos, mustard, oil, and tarragon. Shake to distribute the marinade.

Marinate for as little as 20 minutes, or overnight if you desire.

Preheat the oven to 400°F. Line a rimmed baking sheet with foil.

Arrange the portobellos in a single layer on the baking sheet and spoon half of the marinade over them. Bake for 20 minutes or until soft and tender.

# Roasted Vegetables

*The key to a quick and easy holiday dinner is components like Roasted Vegetables that take just minutes to put together. Once you've got your veggies in the oven, you can set your timer and forget about them, freeing up your time to prepare the rest of your vegan feast.*

**MAKES 4 TO 6 SERVINGS**

3 carrots, peeled and cut into ½-inch coins

2 medium parsnips, peeled and cut into ½-inch coins

1 medium turnip, peeled and cut into 8 wedges

1 medium celery root, peeled and cut into 8 large chunks

¼ cup extra-virgin olive oil

Kosher salt to taste

Freshly ground black pepper to taste

Preheat the oven to 450°F. Line two baking sheets with parchment paper or nonstick foil.

Toss the carrots, parsnips, turnip, and celery root with the olive oil, salt, and pepper. Divide the vegetables evenly among the baking sheets and spread in a single layer. Roast the vegetables, turning about halfway through cooking, until caramelized and tender, 45 to 50 minutes.

# Potato Latkes

MAKES 4 TO 6 SERVINGS

*The key to making these traditional latkes quick and easy is a food processor. Cut the potatoes to fit the size of your food processor chute, then use the shredding/grating blade to make 3 pounds of grated potatoes in less than 5 minutes. Latkes are traditionally served with applesauce.*

3 pounds russet potatoes, peeled and grated

2 egg equivalent prepared Ener-G Egg Replacer (see page 5)

1 teaspoon fine sea salt

3 tablespoons unbleached all-purpose flour

½ teaspoon baking powder

½ medium white or yellow onion, diced

⅛ teaspoon paprika

Freshly ground black pepper to taste

Canola oil for frying

Applesauce

Put the potatoes, prepared egg replacer, salt, flour, baking powder, onion, paprika, and pepper in a large bowl and mix with a spoon or your hands until well combined.

Cover the bottom of a large skillet with oil, no more than about ⅛ inch deep, and warm over medium-high heat. You'll know the oil is ready when you sprinkle a small drop of water on the surface and it pops.

In small batches, spoon the latke mixture ¼ cup at a time into the oil. Use a spatula to flatten them out. Fry until golden brown on both sides, about 3 minutes per side. Drain on paper towels. Serve with applesauce.

# Sweet Potato and Parsnip Latkes

*Latkes are so wonderfully versatile; you can make them out of just about anything. This is one of my favorite sweet and savory combinations. To cut down on your prep time, use the grating blade on your food processor. It also makes grating onions a tear-free experience.*

**MAKES 4 SERVINGS**

½ medium yellow onion

1 small Yukon Gold potato (about ¼ pound), peeled

1 small garnet sweet potato or yam (about ½ pound), peeled

1 medium parsnip, peeled

3 tablespoons unbleached all-purpose flour

1 teaspoon kosher salt

Pinch of cayenne pepper

2 egg equivalent prepared Ener-G Egg Replacer (see page 5)

Canola oil for frying

2 tablespoons chopped flat-leaf parsley

Vegan sour cream, optional

Grate the onion, potato, sweet potato, and parsnip. Put them in a medium bowl and toss to combine. Fold in the flour, salt, cayenne, and prepared egg replacer. Stir until the ingredients are completely combined.

Cover the bottom of a large skillet with oil, no more than about ⅛ inch deep, and warm over medium-high heat. In small batches, spoon the latke mixture ¼ cup at a time into the skillet, pressing lightly to form pancakes. Cook until golden on both sides, about 3 minutes on each side.

Garnish with parsley and a dollop of vegan sour cream if you like.

# Cauliflower Latkes

*Cauliflower holds a special place in my heart. Unlike most children, when I was little I craved cauliflower over any other vegetable. So I jumped at the chance to add a Cauliflower Latke recipe to this book. Play around with the garnishes you use for the finished latkes. I vacillate between sour cream, applesauce, and even horseradish. Start pulling out the condiments in your fridge and finding your favorite as well.*

1 head cauliflower, broken into florets and steamed until soft
¼ cup matzo meal
2 egg equivalent prepared Ener-G Egg Replacer (see page 5)
2 tablespoons minced fresh parsley
¼ teaspoon garlic salt
Freshly ground black pepper to taste
½ cup canola oil

Mash the cauliflower in a large bowl. Fold in the matzo meal, prepared egg replacer, parsley, garlic salt, and pepper.

Warm the oil in a large skillet over medium-high heat. Form the cauliflower mixture into patties, using about ¼ to ⅓ cup of the mixture for each patty, and fry until golden, about 2 minutes per side.

Drain on paper towels. Serve warm.

# Challah

*The Jewish Sabbath traditionally begins with a blessing over the challah. Unfortunately, there is no way to cut down on the preparation time of this Challah, but, trust me, the time is well spent. Leftover Challah makes a sweet and fluffy French Toast (page 231).*

MAKES 12 TO 14 SERVINGS

4 cups unbleached all-purpose flour, plus more for kneading

2 tablespoons sugar

1 teaspoon baking powder

2¼ teaspoons active dry yeast

1 cup water

⅓ cup agave nectar

1 tablespoon white vinegar

2 tablespoons unsweetened applesauce

¼ cup canola oil

1 tablespoon kosher salt

Mix the flour, sugar, baking powder, and yeast in a large bowl and make a well in the center.

Whisk together the water, agave nectar, vinegar, applesauce, oil, and salt in a small bowl and then pour into the well in the flour mixture. Stir until the ingredients are combined into a soft dough.

Turn the dough out onto a lightly floured surface and knead until it is soft and no longer sticky, adding flour, ¼ cup at a time, as necessary.

Lightly oil a large bowl, put the dough in the bowl, and coat lightly with oil. Cover the bowl with a paper towel and set aside until the dough doubles in size, about 1 hour.

Turn the dough out onto a lightly floured surface and knead for approximately 1 minute or until excess air is released. Reshape into a ball and return to the bowl. Cover and set aside until the dough doubles in size again, about 1 hour.

Preheat the oven to 375°F. Line a baking sheet with parchment paper.

Turn the dough out onto a lightly floured surface and divide into 3 equal pieces. Roll and stretch each piece into a rope 12 to 15 inches long. Arrange the ropes side by side on the work surface. Starting at one end, braid the ropes. When the braid is finished, tuck both ends under and pinch to seal. Place the loaf on the prepared baking sheet. Bake until golden brown, about 35 minutes.

# Sufganiyot

During Hanukkah, people of Jewish faith observe the custom of eating fried foods in commemoration of the miracle of the Temple oil. A sufganiyah is a fried donut. Sufganiyot are widely consumed in Israel in the weeks leading up to and including the Hanukkah holiday. Traditionally they are filled with apricot or raspberry jam, but the new generation of recipes includes chocolate, cream filling, and all kinds of other fun, modern takes on the traditional recipe.

**MAKES 20 DONUTS**

2¼ teaspoons active dry yeast

2 tablespoons warm water

¾ cup plain soy, rice, or almond milk

6 tablespoons sugar

½ teaspoon fine sea salt

1 egg equivalent prepared Ener-G Egg Replacer (see page 5)

3 tablespoons shortening

2½ cups unbleached all-purpose flour, plus more for kneading

Canola oil for frying

¾ cup fruit jelly or jam

Confectioners' sugar

Whisk the yeast with the warm water in a large bowl. Let stand for 5 minutes or until foamy.

Add the milk, sugar, salt, prepared egg replacer, shortening, and 1 cup of the flour to the yeast mixture. Beat with an electric mixer on low speed for 1 minute.

Beat in the remaining 1½ cups flour. Knead in the bowl for 2 to 3 minutes or until the dough is smooth and buoyant, adding flour 2 tablespoons at a time, if needed, to get the right consistency.

Cover the bowl with a damp paper towel and allow the dough to double in size, about 1 hour.

Turn the dough out onto a lightly floured surface and roll out to ½-inch thickness. With a biscuit cutter, cut the dough into 2-inch circles, making sure not to twist the biscuit cutter when cutting the circles.

Set the circles aside, uncovered, and let double in size, about 20 minutes.

Preheat a deep fryer to 350°F or put about ½ inch of oil in a large frying pan over medium heat. To test the heat, sprinkle a small drop of water into the oil. When the water begins to pop, the oil is ready.

Fry the sufganiyot in small batches until golden, 1 to 2 minutes, turning as needed. Drain on paper towels.

Fill a pastry bag with the jelly or jam of your choice and inject about 2 to 3 teaspoons of jelly or jam into each donut. Sprinkle with confectioners' sugar.

# Baked Sufganiyot

*The best part of Hanukkah foods is the fact that a lot of them are fried. But no matter how delicious fried foods are, they aren't exactly waistline friendly. If you're looking for a break from all the oil, then you've found the right recipe. These are still light and fluffy like traditional fried jelly donuts, but without the extra calories.*

**MAKES 20 DONUTS**

2¼ teaspoons active dry yeast

2 tablespoons warm water

¾ cup plain soy, rice, or almond milk

¼ cup granulated sugar

½ teaspoon fine sea salt

⅛ teaspoon ground nutmeg

⅛ teaspoon ground cinnamon

1 egg equivalent prepared Ener-G Egg Replacer (see page 5)

3 tablespoons shortening

2¼ cups unbleached all-purpose flour, plus more for kneading

¾ cup fruit jelly or jam

Confectioners' sugar

Whisk the yeast with the warm water in a large bowl. Let stand for 5 minutes or until foamy.

Add the milk, sugar, salt, nutmeg, cinnamon, prepared egg replacer, shortening, and 1 cup of the flour to the yeast mixture. Beat with an electric mixer on low speed for 1 minute.

Beat in the remaining 1¼ cups flour. Knead in the bowl for 2 to 3 minutes or until the dough is smooth and buoyant, adding flour 2 tablespoons at a time, if needed, to get the right consistency.

Cover the bowl with a damp paper towel and allow the dough to double in size, about 1 hour.

Turn the dough out onto a lightly floured surface and roll out to ½-inch thickness. With a biscuit cutter, cut the dough into 2-inch circles, making sure not to twist the biscuit cutter when cutting the circles.

Set the circles aside, uncovered, and let double in size, about 20 minutes.

Preheat the oven to 420°F. Line a baking sheet with parchment paper.

Transfer the dough circles to the prepared baking sheet and bake for 8 to 10 minutes or until golden. Fill a pastry bag with the jelly or jam of your choice and inject about 2 to 3 teaspoons into each donut. Sprinkle with confectioners' sugar.

# Applesauce Donut Holes

*Although sufganiyot are an Israeli tradition, it can be a time-consuming process to wait for the yeast to rise and to form the dough. If you're looking for a quicker and simpler donut pastry, then these big and fluffy applesauce donut holes will hit the spot.*

**MAKES 28 DONUT HOLES**

Canola oil for frying

2¼ cups unbleached all-purpose flour

1½ teaspoons baking powder

½ teaspoon baking soda

½ teaspoon ground cinnamon

¼ teaspoon ground nutmeg

½ teaspoon fine sea salt

½ cup granulated sugar

¼ cup loosely packed light brown sugar

¼ cup plain soy yogurt

1 egg equivalent prepared Ener-G Egg Replacer (see page 5)

2 tablespoons canola oil

¼ cup plain almond, rice, oat, or soy milk

1 cup unsweetened applesauce

Confectioners' sugar

### Cook's Tip

If you are using a deep fryer, your donuts might not always turn on their own and cook on both sides. About 30 to 45 seconds into frying, turn the donut holes over with a fork—it shouldn't take more than a slight nudge to get them to turn and fry on both sides.

Preheat a deep fryer to 350°F or heat about ½ inch of oil in a large frying pan over medium heat. To test the heat, sprinkle a small drop of water onto the oil. When the water begins to pop, the oil is ready.

Stir together the flour, baking powder, baking soda, cinnamon, nutmeg, salt, granulated sugar, and brown sugar in a large bowl.

Whisk the yogurt, prepared egg replacer, oil, milk, and applesauce in a small bowl. Pour the yogurt mixture into the flour mixture and stir to combine. Drop the dough 1 teaspoon at a time into hot oil and fry in small batches for 1 to 2 minutes or until light, fluffy, and golden. Drain on paper towels.

Dust with confectioners' sugar.

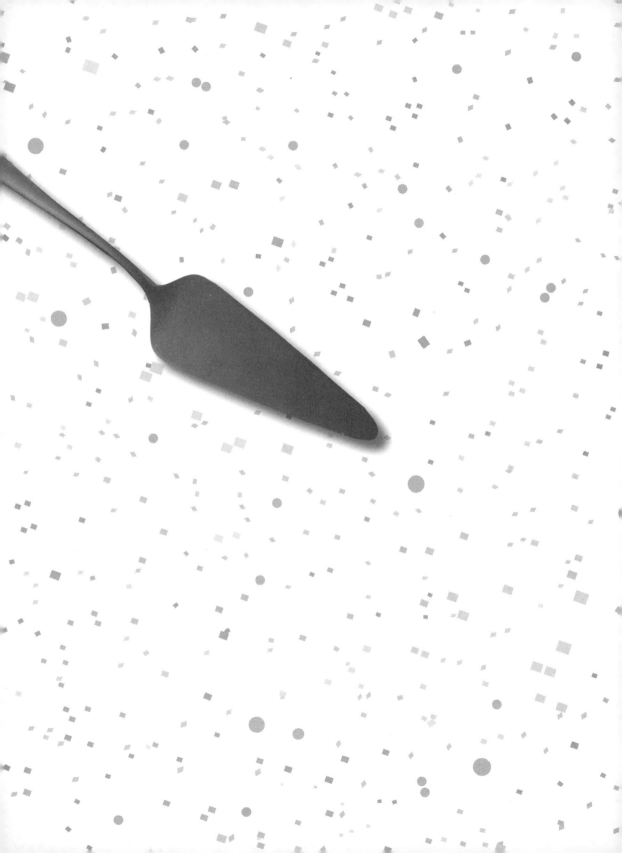

# ★ Christmas ★

**C**HRISTMAS IS THE Christian celebration of the birth of Jesus Christ. It is also a time of year and a holiday packed with more traditions, characters, parties, and presents than nearly any other celebration. It seems like every week in December there's another holiday party, another Secret Santa gift to buy for the office Christmas party, Christmas cards to send to your friends and relatives, gingerbread houses to build and decorate, and pictures to take with Santa and his elves. There's so much to do at Christmastime and so many things that could stress you out, so don't let cooking Christmas dinner or baking up cookies for Santa be one of those stressors too. Here are some quick and easy ways to get your Christmas celebration started off on the right foot.

Christmas Tamales

Hazelnut-Crusted Seitan

Agave-Glazed Acorn Squash

Jamaican Curried Pumpkin Soup

Green Bean Casserole

Dill New Potatoes

Twice-Baked Sweet Potatoes

Mulled Pomegranate Cider

Pecan Fudge

Gingerbread Cookies

Chocolate Macadamia Nut Cookies

Double Chocolate Chip Cookies

Crunchy Cornflake Cookies

# Christmas Tamales

*There's no quick way to make tamales, but as a California girl, there is no way I could open the Christmas season without them. In Mexico, Christmas and tamales go hand in hand, and in my hometown of Fresno, California, the same notion rings true. It simply isn't Christmas without the tamales.*

12 dried corn husks

2 cups masa harina

1 teaspoon fine sea salt

¼ teaspoon garlic powder

½ cup shortening

1½ cups vegetable stock

2 cups steamed fresh or frozen corn

2 cups cooked black beans

2 roasted red bell peppers, diced

2 teaspoons sofrito (see page 10)

3½ teaspoons Taco Seasoning (page 253)

Soak the corn husks in warm water while you prepare the masa and filling.

Mix the masa, salt, and garlic powder in a large bowl. Beat in the shortening with an electric mixer or large spoon. Add the stock ½ cup at a time. Continue to mix with the electric mixer or large spoon, adding stock until you have a consistency that you can spread with a knife.

Stir together the corn, black beans, bell pepper, sofrito, and Taco Seasoning in a medium bowl. One at a time, shake excess water off the corn husks and lay them flat on a work surface.

For each tamale, spread a corn husk evenly with the masa mixture, working it with your hands if you need to. Place a large spoonful of filling on top of the masa, centered on the widest part of the husk.

Fold the long edges of the corn husk to the center over the filling so that they overlap, making sure that none of the filling leaks out. Fold the narrow, unfilled end of the husk up, so that the filling is completely enclosed within the three folded sides.

Place the tamales in a steamer and cook for 40 to 45 minutes. The tamales are cooked when they separate easily from the corn husks.

## Cook's Tip

Depending on the region of the country you live in, corn husks can be difficult to find. Latin-American and international markets nearly always carry corn husks in abundance, so if you don't see them at your local grocer, then try one of these options.

# Hazelnut-Crusted Seitan

MAKES 4 SERVINGS

*When grinding hazelnuts, it is necessary to have a high-quality food processor or Vita-Mix with a dry ingredients blade. I tried, and failed at, grinding my hazelnuts in a little mini food processor the first time, and needless to say the food processor didn't live to see another day. Like the Tourkey Cutlets (page 172), this recipe also pairs well with Sage Gravy (page 248).*

5 tablespoons unbleached all-purpose flour

¾ cup raw hazelnuts

¼ teaspoon garlic powder

¼ teaspoon onion powder

¼ teaspoon fine sea salt

⅛ teaspoon cayenne pepper

½ cup plain hazelnut, soy, rice, or almond milk

1 teaspoon baking powder

¼ cup canola oil

1 recipe Chik'n Seitan (page 258), cut into 4 cutlets

Put 4 tablespoons of the flour and the hazelnuts, garlic powder, onion powder, salt, and cayenne in a food processor and process into a coarse meal. Transfer to a small shallow bowl.

In another small bowl, whisk the milk with the remaining 1 tablespoon flour and the baking powder.

Warm the oil in a large skillet over medium to medium-high heat. Dip the seitan pieces into the milk mixture, then into the hazelnut mixture, and panfry until golden on both sides, about 2 minutes per side.

## Cook's Tip

If you don't have a food processor strong enough to grind hazelnuts, feel free to use preground hazelnuts instead. Use a heaping ½ cup of preground hazelnuts instead of whole hazelnuts for this recipe.

# Agave-Glazed Acorn Squash

*Spring and summer bring luscious sweet berries and bright colorful fruits, but winter yields my favorite array of vegetables—gourds, roots, and various squash. For the longest time, I was intimidated by all forms of roots and gourds. I couldn't figure out how to tackle them, cook them, and bring out their flavor. I decided to dive in headfirst and just buy every type of root, gourd, and squash at the market, bring it home, and experiment. I was shocked at how rich and flavorful they are and how such simple ingredients can produce such a phenomenal flavor. With the addition of just five ingredients, these acorn squash turn into a delicious meal.*

**MAKES 4 SERVINGS**

2 small acorn squash

¼ cup agave nectar

2 tablespoons nonhydrogenated margarine, cut into small pieces

¼ cup chopped pecans

2 tablespoons raisins or sweetened dried cranberries

2 teaspoons vegan Worcestershire sauce

Preheat the oven to 400°F. Line a baking sheet with nonstick foil or parchment paper.

Cut the acorn squash lengthwise into halves. Do not remove the seeds. Place the squash cut side up on the prepared baking sheet. Bake for 30 to 45 minutes or until soft. Leave the oven on. Remove the seeds and fibers.

Mix the agave nectar, margarine, pecans, raisins and Worcestershire sauce and spoon into the squash. Bake for 5 to 10 minutes more or until a light glaze has formed over each squash half.

# Jamaican Curried Pumpkin Soup

MAKES 4 TO 6 SERVINGS

*When one thinks of Christmas, Jamaican flavors usually don't come to mind, and that's why I love this dish so much. It's a nontraditional element that brings a little spice and fun to a traditional Christmas dinner. After all, who determines what's "traditional" anyway?*

1½ cups vegetable stock

One 15-ounce can pumpkin purée

One 14-ounce can unsweetened coconut milk

2 tablespoons agave nectar

1 tablespoon hot Jamaican curry powder

¼ teaspoon ground allspice

¼ teaspoon ground cloves

¼ teaspoon fine sea salt

Freshly ground black pepper to taste

Whisk all the ingredients together in a medium saucepan over medium heat. Cook until heated through, about 10 minutes.

## Cook's Tip

Jamaican curry powder and the typical curry powder you find at the grocery store are not the same set of spices. You can usually find hot Jamaican curry in the ethnic food aisle of your local grocery store or at an international market.

# Green Bean Casserole

*I only use French fried onions once a year, and that's for this Green Bean Casserole. I'm not sure who first thought of frying up onions into crispy, yummy spirals, but whoever you are, sir or madam, I tip my hat to you for helping to make this casserole divine.*

MAKES 4 TO 6 SERVINGS

2 tablespoons canola oil

½ cup chopped cremini or white mushrooms

3 tablespoons unbleached all-purpose flour

½ teaspoon fine sea salt

¼ teaspoon ground black pepper

¼ teaspoon onion powder

1 cup plain soy milk

1½ pounds fresh green beans, cut into 2-inch pieces

1⅓ cups French fried onions

Preheat the oven to 350°F.

Warm the oil in a medium saucepan over medium heat. Add the mushrooms and sauté until they begin to brown, about 2 minutes. Stir in the flour, salt, pepper, and onion powder until incorporated. Slowly whisk in the milk and stir constantly until the mixture begins to bubble and thicken. Cook until thickened, about 5 minutes. Stir in the green beans and ⅔ cup of the fried onions and transfer to a 1½- to 2-quart baking dish.

Bake uncovered for 15 minutes or until the casserole begins to bubble. Remove from the oven, stir, and sprinkle with the remaining ⅔ cup fried onions. Bake for an additional 5 minutes or until the onions are golden.

# Dill New Potatoes

*With just five ingredients and 15 minutes of cooking time, you'll have a no-fuss side dish that is sure to please the whole family.*

8 medium red potatoes, scrubbed

3 tablespoons canola oil

2 garlic cloves, minced

1 tablespoon chopped fresh dill, or 1 teaspoon dried dill

¼ teaspoon fine sea salt

Cut each potato into 8 wedges. Steam the potatoes for 10 to 12 minutes or until tender.

Warm the oil in a large skillet over medium heat. Add the garlic and sauté for 1 minute or until fragrant. Add the potatoes, dill, and salt. Toss gently until the potatoes are coated and serve warm.

# Twice-Baked Sweet Potatoes

*Sweet potatoes are so nice, I just had to bake them twice.*

**MAKES 4 SERVINGS**

2 large garnet sweet potatoes or yams

¼ cup plain oat or rice milk

2 tablespoons light brown sugar

¼ teaspoon ground cinnamon

¼ teaspoon ground nutmeg

¼ cup raisins or dried cranberries, optional

¼ cup chopped pecans

Preheat the oven to 450°F. Line a baking sheet with nonstick foil.

Cut the sweet potatoes in half lengthwise and place them cut side down on the prepared baking sheet. Bake for 30 to 35 minutes or until tender. Leave the oven on.

Scoop the potato flesh into a bowl, leaving ¼ inch of flesh in the shells. Put the milk, sugar, cinnamon, nutmeg, and raisins (if using) into the bowl. Mash with the back of a large spoon or a potato masher until well blended.

Spoon the potato mixture back into shells and top with the chopped pecans. Bake for 10 minutes or until the potatoes are heated through and the nuts are toasted.

# Mulled Pomegranate Cider

*This is the kind of drink you cuddle up with by the fireplace at Christmastime while sharing stories and laughs with family and friends. Feel free to leave out the spiced rum and double up on the mulling spices to make this a kid-friendly cider.*

4 cups pomegranate juice

2½ cups apple cider

1 cup cranberry juice (not cranberry cocktail)

2 cups dark spiced rum

2 tablespoons agave nectar

6 cardamom pods

2 cinnamon sticks

2 teaspoons whole allspice

2 whole star anise

1 teaspoon whole cloves

Stir together all the ingredients in a medium saucepan and warm over low heat, stirring occasionally, for 20 minutes or until fragrant. Strain out the spices and serve warm.

## Sweets for Santa

N O ONE IS quite sure if Santa is vegan or not. But one thing's for sure—after trying this assortment of cookies and sweets, Santa might start making semiannual trips down your chimney to get these sweet treats all year round.

# Pecan Fudge

*What could Santa want more than soft, velvety chocolate fudge? Don't feel confined to using just pecans in your fudge. Experiment with chopped hazelnuts, macadamia nuts, almonds, and Brazil nuts if you'd like.*

**MAKES 2 POUNDS**

½ cup vegan cream cheese

½ cup nonhydrogenated margarine, softened

4 cups confectioners' sugar

1 teaspoon vanilla extract

½ cup unsweetened cocoa powder

⅓ cup chopped pecans

Line an 8-inch square pan with wax paper.

In a food processor, blend the cream cheese and margarine until smooth. Add the confectioners' sugar, vanilla, and cocoa powder and process until smooth.

Transfer the mixture to a medium bowl and work in the nuts.

Press the fudge into the pan, using a knife or metal spatula to spread it evenly. Refrigerate until firm, about 3 hours. Use the edges of the wax paper to lift the fudge out of the pan. Cut the fudge into bite-size pieces. Store, refrigerated, in an airtight container for up to 1 week.

### Cook's Tip

You don't have to wait an hour for your margarine to soften at room temperature—just pop it in the microwave for 10 seconds and it will be perfectly softened.

# Gingerbread Cookies

*Most people gain a celebratory "freshman fifteen" when they enter college, but I managed to gain my fifteen pounds after I graduated and started my first job. Why the sudden weight gain? A weekly delivery of gingerbread men. Whether it was winter, spring, summer, or fall, there was a gingerbread man for every season dressed up in clothes that reflected the season. Those little gingerbread men became my weekly obsession, and now these little gingerbread cookies can be yours.*

½ cup shortening

½ cup sugar

1½ teaspoons baking powder

½ teaspoon baking soda

1 teaspoon ground ginger

½ teaspoon ground cinnamon

¼ teaspoon ground nutmeg

¼ teaspoon ground allspice

½ teaspoon ground cloves

½ cup molasses

¼ cup unsweetened applesauce

1 tablespoon white vinegar

1½ cups unbleached all-purpose flour

1 cup whole wheat pastry flour

1 recipe Cream Cheeze Frosting (page 245)

Preheat the oven to 375°F. Grease a cookie sheet with oil or line with parchment paper.

Cream the shortening and sugar with an electric mixer. Add the baking powder, baking soda, ginger, cinnamon, nutmeg, allspice, cloves, molasses, applesauce, and vinegar and beat until well mixed. Add the flour ½ cup at a time, beating until well incorporated. Divide the dough in half, cover, and chill for at least 1 hour.

Working with half the dough at a time, roll it out on a lightly floured surface to ⅛- to ¼-inch thickness (thinner for crispier cookies). Using a 5- to 6-inch cookie cutter, cut into desired shape. Place 1 to 2 inches apart on the prepared cookie sheet.

Bake the cookies one sheet at a time for 6 to 7 minutes or until the edges are lightly browned. Allow the cookies to cool completely before decorating with the Cream Cheeze Frosting.

# Chocolate Macadamia Nut Cookies

**MAKES ABOUT 36 COOKIES**

*This recipe makes about three dozen cookies. Three dozen cookies is great for a crowd or a very hungry Santa, but if you're making treats for a smaller group you can cut this recipe in half with no problem. Alternatively, you can make the entire recipe and freeze half the dough. Wrap it tightly in plastic wrap and store in an airtight container in the freezer for up to a month.*

2½ cups unbleached all-purpose flour

1 teaspoon baking soda

1 teaspoon baking powder

½ teaspoon fine sea salt

1 cup loosely packed light brown sugar

½ cup granulated sugar

½ cup unsweetened applesauce

2 teaspoons vanilla extract

½ cup nonhydrogenated margarine

½ cup shortening

1 cup vegan semisweet chocolate chips

¾ cup raw macadamia nuts, coarsely chopped

Preheat the oven to 350°F.

Mix the flour, baking soda, baking powder, and salt in a medium bowl.

Cream together the brown sugar, granulated sugar, applesauce, vanilla, margarine, and shortening in a separate medium bowl with an electric mixer.

Beat in the flour mixture ½ cup at a time until completely incorporated. Stir in the chocolate chips and nuts. Cover the bowl and refrigerate for 10 minutes.

Roll about 2 tablespoons of the dough into a ball and place on an ungreased baking sheet about 2 inches apart. Repeat until all the dough is gone. Bake the cookies one sheet at a time for 13 to 15 minutes depending on desired texture. The longer you bake the cookies, the crispier they will become.

# Double Chocolate Chip Cookies

*A true chocolate lover can never get enough, so why not make a chocolate chip cookie with chocolate in the dough? If you're looking for a complete chocolate overload, pour a glass of cold chocolate soy milk to dunk these treasures in.*

**MAKES 24 COOKIES**

2 cups unbleached all-purpose flour

½ cup unsweetened cocoa powder

1 teaspoon baking soda

1 teaspoon baking powder

½ teaspoon fine sea salt

½ cup nonhydrogenated margarine

½ cup shortening

1 cup loosely packed light brown sugar

½ cup granulated sugar

⅓ cup unsweetened applesauce

1 teaspoon vanilla extract

1 cup vegan semisweet chocolate chips

¾ cup raw pecans, chopped

Preheat the oven to 350°F.

Stir the flour, cocoa powder, baking soda, baking powder, and salt in a medium bowl.

Cream together the margarine, shortening, brown sugar, granulated sugar, applesauce, and vanilla with an electric mixer.

Add the flour mixture to the margarine mixture ½ cup at a time, beating well with an electric mixer after each addition until all the flour is incorporated.

Fold in the chocolate chips and pecans. Spoon out 1-inch balls of dough and place on an ungreased cookie sheet 2 inches apart. Bake the cookies one sheet at a time for 13 to 15 minutes depending on desired texture. The longer you bake the cookies, the crispier they will become.

# Crunchy Cornflake Cookies

**MAKES 24 COOKIES**

*Not every treat has to be a well-thought-out decadent dessert. I literally first made these cornflake cookies from a hodgepodge of leftover pantry items that ended up becoming these wonderfully crunchy, buttery treats.*

½ cup nonhydrogenated margarine

½ cup shortening

½ cup granulated sugar

½ cup loosely packed light brown sugar

2 tablespoons unsweetened applesauce

¼ teaspoon vanilla extract

¼ teaspoon fine sea salt

½ teaspoon baking powder

½ teaspoon baking soda

1¾ cups unbleached all-purpose flour

½ cup crushed cornflakes

½ cup quick-cooking oats

½ cup chopped pecans

Preheat the oven to 350°F.

Cream the margarine, shortening, granulated sugar, brown sugar, and applesauce together with an electric mixer.

Fold in the remaining ingredients in the order listed, one at a time.

Form the dough into 1-inch balls and place on an ungreased cookie sheet. Flatten with the tines of a fork.

Bake the cookies one sheet at a time for 10 to 12 minutes, depending on desired texture. The longer you bake the cookies, the crispier they will become.

# ★ Kwanzaa ★

KWANZAA IS A weeklong celebration of African heritage and culture observed by individuals of African descent in America. Each of the seven days of Kwanzaa honors a principle—*Umoja* (unity), *Kujichagulia* (self-determination), *Ujima* (collective work and responsibility), *Ujamaa* (cooperative economics), *Nia* (purpose), *Kuumba* (creativity), and *Imani* (faith). The most important part of Kwanzaa, as with all celebrations, is gathering together with family and friends. For Kwanzaa specifically, gathering together for a meal is an important part of the holiday, and it's a wonderful time to explore the richness and culture behind foods from all around the world. A Kwanzaa feast is typically a combination of traditional dishes from around the continent of Africa, Caribbean classics, and Southern favorites. The food is a celebration of the culinary diversity of people of African descent from around the globe.

Spicy Jerk Seitan

North African Meatballs

Red Lentil Stew

Tempeh Yassa

Tempeh Kuku Paka

Panfried Plantains

Sautéed Collard Greens

Jollof Rice

African Peanut Soup

Roasted Red Pepper Corn Bread

# Spicy Jerk Seitan

**MAKES 4 SERVINGS**

*Spicy Jerk Seitan served with Jollof Rice (page 227) and Pan-fried Plantains (page 225) is one of my favorite Kwanzaa meals, and also one of my favorite meals to make for my friends all year round. Not only is it a delicious flavor combination, but watching each of my friends respond differently to the spicy jerk dipping sauce makes for a night full of entertainment.*

Canola oil for frying
½ cup unbleached all-purpose flour
½ cup whole wheat flour
2 tablespoons Jerk Seasoning (page 254)
1 cup plain soy, hemp, or rice milk
1 recipe Chik'n Seitan (page 258), cut into strips
1 recipe Jerk Dipping Sauce (recipe follows)

Preheat a deep fryer to 375°F or heat about ½ inch oil in a large frying pan over medium heat. To test the heat, sprinkle a small drop of water into the oil. When the water begins to pop, the oil is ready.

Mix the all-purpose flour, whole wheat flour, and jerk seasoning in a shallow dish.

Pour the milk into a separate shallow dish.

Dredge the seitan in the flour mixture, then the milk, and then back in the flour.

Fry in small batches until deep brown on both sides, 2 to 3 minutes. Remove from the oil and drain on paper towels. Serve with the Jerk Dipping Sauce.

# ⭐ Jerk Dipping Sauce

**MAKES ⅔ CUP**

1 tablespoon canola oil

½ cup diced white onion

2 garlic cloves, chopped

2 tablespoons whole allspice

½ cup loosely packed light brown sugar

1 habanero or Scotch bonnet pepper

1 teaspoon dried oregano

½ teaspoon dried thyme

½ teaspoon ground cinnamon

½ teaspoon ground nutmeg

1 tablespoon Bragg Liquid Aminos

½ cup ketchup

Warm the oil in a small skillet over medium heat. Add the onion and sauté for 3 minutes or until translucent. Add the garlic and cook for an additional minute.

While the onion and garlic are cooking, grind the allspice berries in a food processor until the majority of the berries are pulverized.

Add the onion mixture and the remaining ingredients to the food processor and process until smooth.

# North African Meatballs

**MAKES 6 TO 8 SERVINGS**

*If you're looking for an introduction to North African cooking, this is a great place to start. The ingredients are familiar and easy to find, and they yield a sweet yet savory meatball that goes perfectly over quinoa, couscous, or brown rice.*

1 cup dark vegetable stock

1 teaspoon hickory liquid smoke

1 teaspoon vegan Worcestershire sauce

1 cup textured vegetable protein (TVP)

¾ cup unseasoned bread crumbs

1 tablespoon vital wheat gluten

2 tablespoons minced cilantro

1-inch piece fresh ginger, peeled and minced

½ teaspoon ground cumin

2 garlic cloves, minced

7 tablespoons ketchup

¼ teaspoon fine sea salt

¼ teaspoon ground black pepper

Canola oil or canola oil cooking spray

**SAUCE**

1 tablespoon canola oil

½ cup diced white or yellow onion

2 garlic cloves, minced

1 tablespoon fresh lemon juice

¾ cup vegetable stock

One 14-ounce can crushed tomatoes, with juices

1 teaspoon agave nectar

½ teaspoon red pepper flakes

⅛ teaspoon ground cinnamon

¼ teaspoon fine sea salt

Freshly ground black pepper to taste

**TO MAKE THE MEATBALLS:** Bring the stock, liquid smoke, and Worcestershire sauce to a boil in a small pot. Remove from the heat, stir in the TVP, and let sit for 5 minutes.

Mix the bread crumbs, reconstituted TVP, vital wheat gluten, cilantro, ginger, cumin, garlic, ketchup, salt, and pepper in a medium bowl. Bring the mixture together with your hands. Form rounded tablespoons of the mixture into balls and place on a large plate or baking dish. Refrigerate for about 1 hour.

These meatballs can be either panfried or baked. To panfry the meatballs, put just enough canola oil in a medium skillet to fill the bottom. Warm the oil over medium heat and add the meatballs. Cook on all sides until browned, about 10 minutes. Drain on paper towels.

To bake the meatballs, preheat the oven to 350°F. Line a baking sheet with parchment paper. Arrange the meatballs on the baking sheet in a single layer and spray with canola oil. Bake for 20 to 25 minutes or until firm, flipping them halfway through and spraying with canola oil.

**TO MAKE THE SAUCE:** Warm the oil in a large saucepan over medium heat. Add the onion and sauté until soft, about 3 minutes. Add the garlic and sauté for an additional minute. Stir in the lemon juice and cook for 1 minute. Stir in the stock, tomatoes, agave nectar, red pepper flakes, cinnamon, and salt. Simmer for 5 minutes. Season with black pepper.

Add the meatballs to the sauce and stir to coat. Serve hot.

> ### Cook's Tip
> The meatballs can be made 1 to 2 days in advance and refrigerated until you are ready to make the sauce, or you can freeze cooked meatballs (without sauce) for up to 1 month.

# Red Lentil Stew

*This stew has its roots in North Africa. Instead of traditional stovetop slow cooking methods, I suggest using a Crock-Pot or slow cooker to make this dish super easy and ready whenever you are. Serve this with brown or jasmine rice (see page 22).*

2 cups cooked chickpeas

2 pounds butternut squash, peeled, seeded and cut into ½-inch cubes

2 large carrots, peeled and cut into ½-inch pieces

½ medium white or yellow onion, diced

1 cup red lentils

4 cups vegetable stock

2 tablespoons ketchup

2-inch piece fresh ginger, peeled and minced

1 cinnamon stick

½ teaspoon fine sea salt

¼ teaspoon saffron

¼ teaspoon red pepper flakes

½ cup chopped roasted unsalted peanuts

¼ cup chopped cilantro

Put the chickpeas, squash, carrots, onion, lentils, stock, ketchup, ginger, cinnamon, salt, saffron, and red pepper flakes into 6-quart slow cooker and cook on low heat for 4 to 6 hours. Remove the cinnamon stick.

Top with the peanuts and cilantro to serve.

## Cook's Tip

Cutting butternut squash can be pretty time intensive. To reduce your prep time, look for precut or frozen butternut squash.

# Tempeh Yassa

*Yassa is a spicy, tangy dish with origins in Senegambia. Yassa is one of the most popular dishes in West Africa and this particular variation, with lemon and onion, is a specialty in the Casamance region of Senegal.*

MAKES 6 TO 8 SERVINGS

4 tablespoons canola oil

One 8-ounce package tempeh, any variety, sliced thin

½ medium sweet onion, diced

1 habanero or Scotch bonnet pepper, minced

2 medium carrots, diced

4 garlic cloves, minced

1 small cabbage (about 1 pound), cut into thin strips

2 cups vegetable stock

½ cup fresh lemon juice (about 4 large lemons)

2 tablespoons apple cider vinegar

1 bay leaf

2 tablespoons Dijon mustard

2 cups prepared brown rice or couscous

Warm 2 tablespoons of the oil in a large saucepan over medium heat, add the tempeh, and cook until browned on both sides, about 5 minutes.

Remove the tempeh from the pan and set aside. Pour the remaining 2 tablespoons of oil into the saucepan. Add the onion, habanero, carrots, and garlic and sauté for 5 minutes or until the vegetables begin to soften. Stir in the cabbage and stock and cook until the stock is almost completely gone and the cabbage is tender, 7 to 8 minutes.

Add the tempeh back in, along with the lemon juice, vinegar, bay leaf, and mustard, and bring to a low boil.

Reduce the heat and simmer, uncovered, until the sauce thickens, about 10 minutes.

Remove the bay leaf. Serve with brown rice or couscous.

# Tempeh Kuku Paka

MAKES 6 TO 8 SERVINGS

*Kuku Paka is a coconut curry with origins on the coast of East Africa. This is a staple dish in the region and draws from their abundant supply of coconuts.*

2 tablespoons canola oil

½ cup diced white or sweet onion

½ large green bell pepper, diced

1 garlic clove, minced

1-inch piece fresh ginger, peeled and minced

2 teaspoons curry powder

¼ teaspoon ground cloves

½ teaspoon cayenne pepper or red pepper flakes

½ teaspoon fine sea salt

1½ cups vegetable stock

1 large russet or Yukon Gold potato (about ½ pound), scrubbed and diced

Two 8-ounce packages tempeh, any variety, sliced thin

One 14-ounce can petite diced tomatoes, with juices

One 14-ounce can coconut milk

¼ cup chopped fresh cilantro or parsley

2 cups prepared brown rice

Warm the oil in a large soup pot or Dutch oven over medium-high heat. Add the onion and bell pepper and sauté for 3 minutes. Stir in the garlic and ginger and cook for an additional minute.

Add the curry powder, cloves, cayenne, salt, stock, and potatoes. Cover and cook for 10 minutes or until the potatoes are tender.

Stir in the tempeh, tomatoes, and coconut milk and cook, uncovered, for 5 minutes.

Garnish with the cilantro and serve over brown rice.

# Panfried Plantains

*Plantains, or* maduros, *look like large bananas, but have a sweetness that is unmatched by most other bananas. Chances are you've already seen them in your local grocery store and not even realized what they were. They're those black, large, banana-looking fruits sitting in the specialty fruits section. The color of your plantains is very important—the less yellow and the more black they are, the riper and sweeter they will be.*

**MAKES 6 TO 8 SERVINGS**

2 tablespoons canola oil

4 large, very ripe plantains

Warm 1 tablespoon of the oil in a large skillet over medium heat.

Peel the plantains and cut them on a diagonal  into slices about ½-inch thick. Place half the cut plantains in the skillet. Cook for 3 to 4 minutes on each side or until golden brown. Repeat with the remaining oil and plantains.

# Sautéed Collard Greens

**MAKES 4 TO 6 SERVINGS**

*Experiment with these greens by mixing and matching collards with kale, turnip greens, and/or mustard greens.*

1 pound collard greens
3 tablespoons canola oil
3 garlic cloves, minced
Fine sea salt to taste
Freshly ground black pepper to taste

Roll the leaves of the collard greens and slice ½ inch thick until the entire bunch is chopped.

Warm the oil in a medium skillet over medium heat. Add the garlic and sauté until fragrant, about 1 minute. Add the collard greens and cook until they have wilted down and are bright green, about 5 minutes. Season with salt and pepper.

# Jollof Rice

*Jollof Rice is an amazingly flavorful West African dish with origins in Mali. This version utilizes whole-grain quick brown rice to cut down on cooking time. Look for brown rice with a 10-minute cooking time (see page 22).*

MAKES 8 TO 10 SERVINGS

2 tablespoons canola oil

¾ cup diced white or yellow onions

1 large red bell pepper, diced

4 garlic cloves, minced

1 medium carrot, diced

1 serrano chile, minced

One 14-ounce can petite diced tomatoes, with juices

3 tablespoons tomato paste

1 cup fresh or frozen and thawed green beans, cut into 1-inch pieces

3½ cups vegetable stock

2 cups quick-cooking brown rice

½ teaspoon fine sea salt

### Cook's Tip

Handle hot peppers like serranos with gloves to ensure that you don't get any of the juices under your nails. Take it from experience, rubbing your eyes with serrano juice on your fingers is no picnic.

Warm the oil in a large skillet over medium heat. Add the onions, bell pepper, garlic, carrot, and serrano chile and sauté for 5 minutes. Stir in the tomatoes, tomato paste, green beans, and 1 cup of the stock. Bring to a boil, reduce the heat, and simmer for 5 minutes. Stir in the remaining 2½ cups stock and the rice. Simmer for 12 to 15 minutes, or until all the liquid has been absorbed. Stir in the salt and serve.

# African Peanut Soup

*African Peanut Soup merges every corner of the produce section into one creamy, spicy, yet sweet soup. The first time I made this soup I sat down and ate the entire four servings by myself in one day. This soup is not only great for a Kwanzaa feast but is also a wonderful use of seasonal autumn vegetables that warms you up from the inside out throughout the fall and winter.*

1 tablespoon canola oil

½-inch piece fresh ginger, peeled and chopped

2 medium to large carrots, peeled and chopped

1 large yellow bell pepper, chopped

1 serrano chile pepper, chopped

2 garlic cloves, chopped

½ medium white or yellow onion, chopped

1 medium garnet sweet potato or yam, peeled and chopped

3 cups vegetable stock

½ cup creamy peanut butter

One 8-ounce can tomato sauce

½ cup chopped roasted peanuts

Warm the oil in a large saucepan over medium heat. Add the ginger, carrots, bell pepper, serrano chile, garlic, and onion. Sauté for 5 minutes, then stir in the sweet potato and stock.

Bring the soup to a boil, reduce the heat, and simmer, covered, for 10 minutes.

Transfer the soup to a blender, add the peanut butter, and purée until smooth.

Return the purée to the saucepan and stir in the tomato sauce. Cook until warmed through. Transfer to servings bowls and top with the peanuts.

# Roasted Red Pepper Corn Bread

*My preference is to bake this corn bread in a well-seasoned cast-iron skillet, but a 9-inch-round cake pan will do fine.*

**MAKES 6 TO 8 SERVINGS**

1¾ cups cornmeal

1 cup unbleached all-purpose flour or white rice flour

3 tablespoons sugar

1½ tablespoons baking powder

1 teaspoon fine sea salt

3 tablespoons white vinegar

1½ cups plain rice milk or unsweetened almond milk

½ cup canola oil

¾ cup grated vegan cheddar

1 cup fresh or frozen and thawed corn

1 roasted red bell pepper, diced

1 green onion, chopped

Preheat the oven to 400°F. Grease a cast-iron skillet, 2-quart casserole dish, or 9-inch cake pan with shortening or oil.

Mix the cornmeal, flour, sugar, baking powder, and salt in a large bowl. Make a well in the center and add the vinegar, milk, and canola oil. Stir until combined. Fold in the cheese, corn, bell pepper, and green onion.

Pour the batter into the prepared baking dish. Bake for 40 minutes or until golden and a toothpick comes out clean.

# ★ Birthday Sweets ★

**H**APPY BIRTHDAY TO you! No matter what you whip up as your birthday breakfast, lunch, or dinner, the best part of any birthday is the sweets. You can't very well put a candle on Hazelnut-Crusted Seitan (page 204) and make a wish—well, you could if you wanted to, but what would be the fun in that?! Here's a collection of cakes, cupcakes, cookies, and ice cream to ensure that, no matter how you start your birthday, you'll end it with a sugar rush.

French Toast with Maple Ice Cream

Carrot Cake with Cream Cheeze Frosting

Classic White Cake with Buttercream Frosting

Key Lime Cupcakes

Golden Cupcakes with Chocolate Cream Cheeze Frosting

Cheesecake

Vanilla Bean Ice Cream

Sweet Agave Frozen Yogurt

# French Toast with Maple Ice Cream

**MAKES 4 SERVINGS**

*It's your birthday, so why not find a way to sneak in decadent desserts throughout the entire day? If there was ever a day to do it, today's the day!*

1 cup plain soy or oat milk

¼ cup chickpea flour

¼ teaspoon ground cinnamon

¼ teaspoon ground nutmeg

½ teaspoon vanilla extract

6 slices whole-grain spelt bread or Challah (page 193)

1 recipe Maple Ice Cream (recipe follows)

In a shallow dish, whisk together the milk and chickpea flour. Once the flour is well incorporated, whisk in the cinnamon, nutmeg, and vanilla until thoroughly combined. There will be little lumps left in the batter. Don't worry about them too much, just make sure the bigger ones are dissolved.

Heat a large skillet over medium heat and add enough oil to cover the bottom of the pan. The canola oil will be very important throughout this process. You will learn by trial and error what is too much or too little. Remember that the bread will absorb some of the oil, so add a little extra in preparation for that.

Dredge each slice of bread in the milk mixture and add to the hot oil. Cook until each side is golden brown, 2 to 3 minutes per side. Serve with the Maple Ice Cream.

## Maple Ice Cream

**MAKES 1 QUART**

1½ cups plain soy milk

½ cup Grade A maple syrup

2 tablespoons light brown sugar

1½ cups plain soy yogurt

1 teaspoon vanilla extract

Whisk the milk with the sugar and maple syrup until the sugar is completely dissolved. Whisk the soy yogurt and vanilla into the milk mixture.

Pour the mixture into an electric ice cream maker and freeze according to the manufacturer's directions. This usually takes 25 to 30 minutes to freeze.

# Carrot Cake with Cream Cheeze Frosting

*Café Sunflower in Atlanta, Georgia, has the most amazing vegan carrot cake you will ever taste. For my twenty-ninth birthday there was nothing I wanted more than their delicious carrot cake. However, at over $5 a slice it can get pretty pricey to buy an entire cake (but well worth it as an occasional indulgence). This is my version of their sweet, decadent carrot cake.*

1 cup whole wheat pastry flour

1¼ cups unbleached all-purpose flour

¼ teaspoon fine sea salt

1½ teaspoons baking powder

1¼ teaspoons baking soda

¼ teaspoon ground nutmeg

¼ teaspoon ground cinnamon

½ teaspoon ground ginger

¼ cup plain rice milk

½ cup unsweetened applesauce

1 tablespoon apple cider vinegar

1 cup agave nectar

¼ cup sugar

1 teaspoon vanilla extract

2 large carrots, shredded

¾ cup nonhydrogenated margarine, softened

1 cup chopped pecans or walnuts

1 recipe Cream Cheeze Frosting (page 246)

Preheat the oven to 350°F. Grease a 9-inch cake pan or spring-form pan with shortening.

Stir together the whole wheat pastry flour, all-purpose flour, salt, baking powder, baking soda, nutmeg, cinnamon, and ginger and set aside.

Stir together the milk, applesauce, vinegar, agave nectar, sugar, and vanilla in a medium bowl. Beat in 1 cup of the flour mixture, the carrots, and the margarine with an electric mixer until combined. Beat in the remainder of the flour mixture and then fold in the chopped nuts.

Pour the batter into the prepared pan and bake for 45 to 50 minutes or until the cake is golden brown and a toothpick comes out clean.

Remove the cake from the oven and allow to cool in the pan for 10 minutes. Whether using a springform pan or cake pan, run a knife or spatula around the edges of the pan to loosen the cake. If using a cake pan, invert the cake onto a serving plate and allow to cool completely before icing. If using a springform pan, simply unfasten the sides of the pan and remove the cake. When the cake is completely cool, frost with Cream Cheeze Frosting.

# Classic White Cake with Buttercream Frosting

**MAKES 8 TO 10 SERVINGS**

*Key Lime Cupcakes (page 238) and birthday breakfasts of French Toast with Maple Ice Cream (page 231) are decadent and unique additions to a birthday celebration, but sometimes there's nothing better than just a Classic White Cake with Buttercream Frosting. To add a little punch of color and excitement to this cake, add a couple drops of your choice of food coloring to the frosting. You can also get creative by topping the cake with seasonal berries and fruit—it's always nice to attempt to add a healthy touch, even on a day of sugary goodness.*

2 cups unbleached all-purpose flour

1½ teaspoons baking powder

½ teaspoon baking soda

¼ teaspoon fine sea salt

½ cup nonhydrogenated margarine, softened, or shortening

1½ cups sugar

¼ cup unsweetened applesauce

¼ cup plain soy yogurt

1 teaspoon vanilla extract

1⅓ cups plain soy, rice, almond, or oat milk

1 recipe Buttercream Frosting (recipe follows)

Preheat the oven to 350°F. Grease two 8- or 9-inch cake pans with shortening.

Mix the flour, baking powder, baking soda, and salt in a medium bowl.

In a separate bowl, cream the margarine and sugar with an electric mixer, then slowly incorporate the applesauce, yogurt, and vanilla.

Add the sugar mixture plus ⅓ cup of the milk to the flour mixture and beat until combined. Add the remaining milk ⅓ cup at a time, beating well after each addition, until the milk is completely incorporated.

236

Divide the batter evenly between the prepared pans and bake for 25 to 30 minutes or until a toothpick comes out clean. Cool the cakes in their pans for 10 minutes, then remove them from their pans and cool completely before icing with the Buttercream Frosting.

# ★Buttercream Frosting

**MAKES 2½ CUPS**

6 tablespoons shortening

6 tablespoons nonhydrogenated margarine, softened

¼ cup plain soy or rice milk

1 teaspoon vanilla extract

½ teaspoon almond extract (optional)

3½ cups confectioners' sugar

Cream the shortening and margarine with an electric mixer, then add the milk, vanilla, and almond extract (if using). Beat in the confectioners' sugar 1 cup at a time until completely incorporated.

# Key Lime Cupcakes

**MAKES 16 CUPCAKES**

*When I lived in Philadelphia, one of my good friends had an unhealthy obsession with Key lime pie and asked for it on every special occasion. Don't get me wrong—I love Key lime pie just as much as the next girl, but cupcakes are my first love of the dessert world. These cupcakes bridge the divide in one little sweet, tangy treat.*

1¾ cups unbleached all-purpose flour

2 teaspoons baking powder

¼ teaspoon fine sea salt

1¼ cups sugar

½ cup nonhydrogenated margarine, softened

¼ cup plain soy yogurt

¼ cup unsweetened applesauce

3 tablespoons fresh lime juice

2 drops green food coloring

¾ cup plain oat, rice, or soy milk

1 recipe Key Lime Frosting (recipe follows)

Preheat the oven to 350°F. Line two 12-cup cupcake tins with 16 paper baking cups.

Mix the flour, baking powder, and salt in a small bowl.

Cream together the sugar, margarine, yogurt, applesauce, lime juice, and food coloring in a medium bowl with an electric mixer. Beat in ½ cup of the flour mixture, then ¼ cup of the milk, alternately adding each until all the flour and milk are incorporated.

Pour the batter evenly into the cupcake cups and bake one pan at a time for 20 minutes or until a toothpick comes out clean. Allow the cupcakes to cool in the pan for 5 minutes, then remove them from the pan and cool completely before frosting with the Key Lime Frosting.

# Key Lime Frosting

**MAKES 2 CUPS**

One 8-ounce package vegan cream cheese

1½ cups confectioners' sugar

¼ cup shortening

¼ cup nonhydrogenated margarine, softened

1 tablespoon fresh lime juice

½ teaspoon vanilla extract

Beat all the ingredients with an electric mixer until smooth and fluffy. Spread evenly over completely cooled cupcakes.

## Cook's Tip

These cupcakes can be made with regular limes, but if you run across Key limes, definitely use them.

# Golden Cupcakes
## with Chocolate Cream Cheeze Frosting

*These golden little treats are super moist, buttery, and sweet. Once they're topped off with Chocolate Cream Cheeze Frosting, you won't be able to keep your hands off these cupcakes.*

⅓ cup nonhydrogenated margarine, softened

¾ cup plus 2 tablespoons sugar

1 teaspoon vanilla extract

¾ cup plain rice milk

1 tablespoon white vinegar

1¼ cups unbleached all-purpose flour

2¼ teaspoons baking powder

¼ teaspoon fine sea salt

1 tablespoon cornstarch

1 recipe Chocolate Cream Cheeze Frosting (recipe follows)

Preheat the oven to 350°F. Line a cupcake tin with paper baking cups.

Cream the margarine, sugar, and vanilla with an electric mixer on medium-high speed. Stir in the milk and vinegar.

Add the flour, baking powder, salt, and cornstarch and beat until smooth. Divide the batter evenly among the cupcake cups and bake for 20 to 22 minutes or until a toothpick comes out clean. Cool completely before frosting with the Chocolate Cream Cheese Frosting.

# ★ Chocolate Cream Cheeze Frosting

**MAKES 2 CUPS**

½ cup vegan cream cheese

¼ cup nonhydrogenated margarine

2 tablespoons shortening

¼ cup unsweetened cocoa powder

1 teaspoon vanilla extract

3 cups confectioners' sugar

Cream together the cream cheese, margarine, shortening, cocoa powder, and vanilla with an electric mixer on medium speed. If your electric mixer has a whisk attachment, use it for best results. Beat in the confectioners' sugar 1 cup at a time until completely incorporated.

This frosting can be stored for up to 1 week in an airtight container in the refrigerator.

# Cheesecake

*While most people couldn't imagine a birthday celebration without a cake or cupcakes, my best friend can't imagine his without a cheesecake. He's been pestering me to make a vegan cheesecake for years, and, finally, I've decided to oblige. Happy Birthday!*

½ cup raw pecans

½ cup raw almonds

12 graham crackers

6 tablespoons nonhydrogenated margarine, melted

Three 8-ounce packages vegan cream cheese

1¼ cups sugar

One 12.3-ounce package firm silken tofu

2 cups vegan sour cream

2 tablespoons cornstarch or potato starch

1 teaspoon vanilla extract

## Cook's Tip

This is one of those recipes that is easy but not necessarily quick. To maximize your time, I recommend making this first thing in the morning if you plan on serving it in the evening, or making it at night if you plan on serving it the next morning or afternoon. Better yet, make it an entire day ahead of time, giving the cake a full 24 hours to chill. The longer the cake sits, the better the flavor.

Preheat the oven to 350°F. Grease a 9-inch springform pan with margarine or shortening.

Pulse the pecans, almonds, and graham crackers in a food processor until they resemble a dark cornmeal. Transfer the graham cracker mixture to a small bowl and pour in the melted margarine, mixing well.

Press the mixture into prepared springform pan, lining the bottom and sides of the pan.

Put the cream cheese, sugar, tofu, sour cream, cornstarch, and vanilla into a blender and blend until smooth. Pour the mixture on top of the prepared crust and smooth the top with a spatula.

Bake for 60 minutes. Turn off the heat and let the cheesecake sit in the oven for 1 hour with the door closed. Refrigerate the cheesecake for 4 to 24 hours. Remove from the pan when you are ready to serve it.

# Vanilla Bean Ice Cream

*Vanilla extract is a great all-purpose baking and cooking in-gredient, but when it comes to ice cream nothing beats the taste of using the seeds of a vanilla bean.*

**MAKES 1 QUART**

1 vanilla bean, split lengthwise
1½ cups plain soy milk
½ cup plus 2 tablespoons sugar
1½ cups plain soy yogurt

Scrape the seeds out of the vanilla bean with a spoon.

Whisk the milk with the sugar until the sugar is completely dissolved. Whisk in the soy yogurt, then whisk in the vanilla seeds, leaving no lumps.

Pour the mixture into an electric ice cream maker and freeze according to the manufacturer's directions. This usually takes 25 to 30 minutes to freeze.

# Sweet Agave Frozen Yogurt

**MAKES 1 QUART**

*Cake and ice cream are the hallmarks of any birthday celebration. At one point it seemed that between the cake, the frosting, and the ice cream, I would go through at least a 5-pound bag of sugar with every birthday that rolled around. Then in walked agave nectar. It provides all of the sweetness of sugar without the quick sugar rush. If you want all the sweetness with none of the sugar on your next birthday, try Sweet Agave Frozen Yogurt paired with agave-sweetened Carrot Cake (page 234).*

1 vanilla bean, split lengthwise
2 cups plain soy yogurt
1 cup plain soy milk
½ cup agave nectar

Scrape the seeds out of the vanilla bean with a spoon.

Whisk all the ingredients together in a medium bowl.

Pour the mixture into an electric ice cream maker and freeze according to the manufacturer's directions. This usually takes 25 to 30 minutes to freeze.

## Cook's Tip

The key to making a good frozen yogurt is, of course, the yogurt. You want a blank slate to work on, and not all soy yogurts are the same. My preference is Wildwood Farms plain soy yogurt. It has a light taste that is the perfect platform on which to build your flavors.

# ★ The Basics ★

**H**ERE ARE ALL the sauces, dips, gravies, seasoning mixes, and, most importantly, the seitan recipe you'll need to complete all your favorite dishes and make your celebration complete.

Cream Cheeze Frosting

Cheeze Sauce

Sage Gravy

Dill Dip

Thousand Island Dressing

Ranch Dip

Teriyaki Dip

Taco Seasoning

Jerk Seasoning

Cajun Spice Blend

Smokey Maple BBQ Sauce

Pizza Sauce

Chik'n Seitan

# Cream Cheeze Frosting

**MAKES 2 CUPS**

*This is a great basic frosting recipe that goes well on Gingerbread Cookies (page 212), Carrot Cake (page 234), Red Velvet Cupcakes (page 70), and Green Velvet Cupcakes (page 110).*

½ cup vegan cream cheese

¼ cup nonhydrogenated margarine

1 teaspoon vanilla extract

3 cups confectioners' sugar

Beat the cream cheese, margarine, and vanilla with an electric mixer on high speed until light and fluffy. Beat in the confectioners' sugar 1 cup at a time until all the sugar is incorporated. Cover and store refrigerated for up to 1 week.

# Cheeze Sauce

It seems like almost every vegan cheeze sauce out there has soy or nutritional yeast in it. Don't get me wrong—I could eat an entire block of tofu with just salt and pepper and sprinkle nutritional yeast on just about everything, but every once in a while I need a break. Too much of one thing is never good. This Cheeze Sauce is not only rich, creamy, and cheesy, but also soy and gluten free.

**MAKES 3 CUPS**

1 medium Yukon Gold potato, peeled and diced

1 medium carrot, peeled and diced

½ cup diced white onion

1 garlic clove, chopped

1 cup water

½ cup cooked navy beans

¼ cup canola oil

¾ teaspoon fine sea salt

1 tablespoon fresh lemon juice

½ cup raw cashews

Put the potato, carrot, onion, garlic, and water in a small saucepan over medium heat. Bring to a boil, lower the heat, and simmer, covered, for 10 minutes, or until the vegetables are tender. The smaller you cut the vegetables, the less time it will take to cook them.

Put the navy beans, oil, salt, lemon juice, cashews, and cooked vegetables with their cooking water into a blender and process until completely smooth.

# Sage Gravy

*What's a holiday without a gravy boat on the table? Sage Gravy is always a crowd-pleaser and goes great on Tourkey Cutlets (page 172), Crispy Baked Tofu (page 120), Hazelnut-Crusted Seitan (page 204), and just about anything else you can imagine.*

1 cup water

¼ cup unbleached all-purpose flour

1 cup vegetable stock

¼ cup nutritional yeast

4 teaspoon, Bragg Liquid Aminos

½ teaspoon onion powder

1 tablespoon dried sage (not ground)

½ teaspoon dried thyme

Whisk the water with the flour in a medium saucepan over medium heat until the majority of the lumps have been whisked out.

Whisk in the remaining ingredients and bring to a low boil. Reduce the heat and simmer until the desired thickness is achieved.

*Dill is the main attraction of this dip, so don't try to cut corners by using dried dill. The flavor just won't be the same.*

1 cup vegan sour cream

1 cup vegan mayonnaise

1 teaspoon original Spike Seasoning

1 teaspoon onion powder

1 tablespoon chopped fresh dill

2 tablespoons minced fresh parsley

In a small bowl, stir together all the ingredients until well blended. Cover the bowl and chill for at least 2 hours or overnight.

# Thousand Island Dressing

**MAKES 1½ CUPS**

*Not only has Thousand Island Dressing been my favorite salad dressing since 1989, but it is also one of the best sandwich dressings you will ever try. Try it on Tempeh Reuben Sandwiches (page 106) or any of your favorite sandwiches when you're looking for a break from the ordinary.*

1 cup vegan mayonnaise

¼ cup ketchup

1 tablespoon white vinegar

1 tablespoon agave nectar

4 teaspoons sweet pickle relish

½ teaspoon onion powder

⅛ teaspoon fine sea salt

Pinch of freshly ground black pepper

Whisk all the ingredients together in a small bowl. Cover and refrigerate for at least 1 hour but preferably overnight. Store in an airtight container in the refrigerator for up to 1 week.

# Ranch Dip

*A high-speed blender is really needed to get this dip perfectly smooth and creamy, but if you don't happen to have one on hand, try soaking the nuts overnight to soften them up a bit; you should get a creamier texture.*

½ cup raw cashews

1 cup raw macadamia nuts

3 tablespoons fresh lemon juice

2 to 3 garlic cloves, chopped

⅓ cup chopped celery

1 teaspoon dried or 1 tablespoon chopped fresh dill

1 to 1½ teaspoons fine sea salt

1½ teaspoons onion powder

¾ cup plus 2 tablespoons water

Put all the ingredients in a high-powered blender and blend until smooth.

# Teriyaki Dip

*Teriyaki Dip is a sweet, savory, and slightly thicker version of traditional teriyaki sauce. Use it as a dip for Beer-Battered Green Beans (page 36) or any other vegetables of your choosing.*

1¼ cups water

¼ cup Bragg Liquid Aminos

1 tablespoon rice vinegar

¼ teaspoon ground ginger

3 tablespoons agave nectar

2 garlic cloves, minced

2 tablespoons cornstarch or arrowroot

Whisk together 1 cup of the water and the liquid aminos, rice vinegar, ginger, agave nectar, and garlic in a small saucepan and bring to a boil over medium to medium-high heat, stirring constantly.

Dissolve the cornstarch in the remaining ¼ cup water and whisk into the sauce. Continue to cook and stir until sauce has thickened, about 3 to 5 minutes.

*I used to adore a particular store-bought brand of taco season-ing until I looked on the back and realized there were a couple questionable ingredients that I couldn't quite pronounce, not to mention loads of MSG. Thankfully, it is quick and easy to make taco seasoning at home with common herbs, spices, and seasonings.*

**MAKES ⅓ CUP**

3 tablespoons chili powder

1 teaspoon garlic powder

1 teaspoon onion powder

¼ teaspoon cayenne pepper or red pepper flakes

2 teaspoons paprika

2 tablespoons ground cumin

1 teaspoon fine sea salt

½ teaspoon ground black pepper

Mix together all the ingredients in a small bowl. Store in an airtight container.

# Jerk Seasoning

*Jerk seasoning is typically associated with fiery hot spices, but there's no hard-and-fast rule that it has to be a five-alarm fire in your mouth. This seasoning mix is a bit spicy but also very sweet and works perfectly for recipes like Spicy Jerk Seitan (page 218).*

1 teaspoon onion powder

2 teaspoons dried thyme

½ teaspoon dried oregano

1 teaspoon dried parsley

1 teaspoon ground allspice

¼ teaspoon ground cinnamon

½ teaspoon ground black pepper

½ teaspoon cayenne pepper

1 teaspoon paprika

½ teaspoon red pepper flakes

¼ teaspoon ground cumin

1 teaspoon garlic powder

1 teaspoon fine sea salt

¼ teaspoon ground nutmeg

2 teaspoons light brown sugar

Mix all the ingredients in an airtight container and store until ready to use.

# Cajun Spice Blend

Cajun spice blends are built from a plethora of spices from all around the world and grab influences from French, American, and Spanish cultures, just to name a few. All Cajun spice blends are simply a base to help build a bounty of flavor into the dish. This spice blend is slightly smokey, with mild heat. Once you've cooked Cajun food a few times, you'll learn to adjust the heat, smokiness, and even sweetness of this blend to suit your palate.

½ teaspoon ground black pepper

1 teaspoon ground cumin

½ teaspoon celery salt

1 tablespoon dried thyme

1½ teaspoons dried sage

1 tablespoon dried basil

1 tablespoon dried oregano

1 tablespoon dried parsley

1½ teaspoons dry mustard

½ teaspoon red pepper flakes

1½ teaspoons ground ancho chile

1 teaspoon cayenne pepper

1½ tablespoons paprika

½ teaspoon ground nutmeg

Put all the ingredients in a food processor and process until ground into a fine powder. Store in an airtight container until ready to use.

# Smokey Maple BBQ Sauce

**MAKES 1¾ CUPS**

*It is so easy to make homemade BBQ sauce, and this one will knock your knee socks off. It's sweet, tangy, and smokey and goes well on BBQ Tempeh Hoagies with Chipotle Mayo (page 148) or on store-bought veggie burgers.*

1 tablespoon canola oil

½ cup diced white onion

2 garlic cloves, minced

1 cup ketchup

¾ cup Grade A maple syrup

2 tablespoons vegan Worcestershire sauce

½ teaspoon hickory liquid smoke

¼ teaspoon red pepper flakes

Warm the canola oil in a small saucepan over medium heat. Add the onion and sauté until translucent, about 3 minutes. Add the garlic and sauté until fragrant, about 1 minute.

Stir in the ketchup, maple syrup, Worcestershire sauce, liquid smoke, and red pepper flakes.

Reduce the heat, cover, and simmer for 30 minutes. This sauce can be stored for up to 1 week in the refrigerator in an airtight container.

# Pizza Sauce

*Forty-five minutes might seem like a long time to simmer a pizza sauce, but as you taste it throughout the cooking process you'll see how the flavor develops over time. This sauce usually makes enough for two large pizzas, so I like to freeze 1 cup of it to use later.*

One 14.5-ounce can diced tomatoes, with juices
One 6-ounce can tomato paste
½ teaspoon onion powder
½ teaspoon garlic powder
½ teaspoon dried thyme
½ teaspoon dried rosemary
1 teaspoon dried oregano
½ teaspoon fine sea salt
1 teaspoon sugar
¼ teaspoon ground black pepper
1 bay leaf
1 teaspoon fennel seed

Put the diced tomatoes and tomato paste in a blender and blend until smooth. Transfer to a medium saucepan, stir in the remaining ingredients, and bring to a simmer over medium heat. Reduce the heat to low, cover, and simmer for 45 minutes to 1 hour, stirring occasionally. Remove the bay leaf and use the sauce as desired.

# Chik'n Seitan

*Seitan makes the world a better place. If you don't believe me, just try this recipe.*

## BROTH

2½ cups water

¼ cup nutritional yeast

2 tablespoons Bragg Liquid Aminos

1 teaspoon onion powder

1 heaping teaspoon dried sage (not ground)

½ teaspoon dried thyme

¼ teaspoon dried oregano

## SEITAN

½ cup vital wheat gluten

¼ cup soy flour

½ cup water

**TO MAKE THE BROTH:** Put the 2½ cups of water and the nutritional yeast, liquid aminos, onion powder, sage, thyme, and oregano in a medium saucepan and bring to a boil.

**TO MAKE THE SEITAN:** Mix the vital wheat gluten and soy flour in a small bowl, then add the remaining ½ cup water and stir until it forms a ball.

On a lightly floured surface, knead the dough for a little less than 1 minute, then flatten to ½ inch thick.

Cut into desired shape (strips, nuggets, "breasts," and so on). Keep in mind that during the cooking process the seitan will double in size.

Add the seitan to the saucepan one piece at a time, being careful not to splash the hot broth. Reduce the heat, cover, and simmer until all the broth has been absorbed (about 40 to 50 minutes), stirring every 10 minutes. Smaller cuts like nuggets require less time, so keep an eye on them.

### Cook's Tip

This is an excellent make-ahead recipe. Make this up to 3 days ahead of time and store in the refrigerator until ready to use. It also freezes well.

# Acknowledgments

**T**HANK YOU TO the two most inspiring and influential people in my life, my parents, John and Linda. Thank you for believing in me and supporting me through all of life's triumphs and challenges. To my grandmother, Georgianne Little, my number one saleswoman! You are truly irreplaceable and, as the dedication in *Quick and Easy Vegan Comfort Food* says, you inspire me. I love you.

Matthew, thank you again for taking this ride with me and helping me churn out not one but two amazing cookbooks. This experience has been beyond a dream come true. To Pauline and all the folks at Neuwirth & Associates, thank you for designing yet another beautiful book.

Thank you to Lori Maffei for producing yet another set of beautiful food photos for this book.

"Thank you! Thank you! Thank you!" to Rachel Hallows (super tester extraordinaire), Anne Marie Tyler, Jackie Smith, Joan Farkas, Karyn Casper, Amey F. Mathews, Kimberlee Redman, and Luciana Rushing, my phenomenal testers who worked with me at a grueling pace through record-breaking snowstorms, big moves, and major life events to ensure that every recipe was as near perfect as possible. Thank you for consuming more cupcakes than any one person should have to in a lifetime, and for being so patient with my flubs and typos.

Most importantly thank you to all the phenomenal folks who bought my first book, *Quick and Easy Vegan Comfort Food*, which has led me to this new adventure. I read all your emails, tweets, messages, and posts, and I appreciate your support more than you'll ever know.

# Index

# About the Author

**Alicia C. Simpson** has been cooking since she was tall enough to reach the stove. She is the founder of Lici's Sweet Treats Organic Bakery in Atlanta and the creator of the popular Vegan Guinea Pig blog. She has been featured in the documentary *I'm Vegan*. Alicia's first book, *Quick and Easy Vegan Comfort Food*, was published in 2009. She lives in Atlanta.

www.aliciacsimpson.com